MW00572546

Unison Parenting

Unison Parenting

The Comprehensive Guide to Navigating
Christian Parenthood with One Voice

Cecil Taylor

NASHVILLE

NEW YORK • LONDON • MELBOURNE • VANCOUVER

Unison Parenting

The Comprehensive Guide to Navigating Christian Parenthood with One Voice

© 2025 Cecil Taylor

All rights reserved. No portion of this book may be reproduced, stored in a retrieval system, or transmitted in any form or by any means—electronic, mechanical, photocopy, recording, scanning, or other—except for brief quotations in critical reviews or articles, without the prior written permission of the publisher.

Published in New York, New York, by Morgan James Publishing. Morgan James is a trademark of Morgan James, LLC. www.MorganJamesPublishing.com

Proudly distributed by Publishers Group West®

Please note the information contained within this document is for educational and entertainment purposes only. No warranties of any kind are declared or implied. Each family's situation is unique, and the advice and strategies contained herein may not be suitable for your situation. By reading this document, the reader agrees that under no circumstances is the author responsible for any losses, direct or indirect, that are incurred as a result of the use of the information contained within this document, including, but not limited to, errors, omissions, or inaccuracies.

All Scripture quotations are taken from the Holy Bible, New International Version®, NIV®. Copyright © 1973, 1984, 2011 by Biblica, Inc.™ Used by permission of Zondervan. All rights reserved worldwide. www.zondervan.com. The "NIV" and "New International Version" are trademarks registered in the United States Patent and Trademark Office by Biblica, Inc.™ The text was taken from BibleGateway.com.

Morgan James BOGO™

A **FREE** ebook edition is available for you or a friend with the purchase of this print book.

[_____]

CLEARLY SIGN YOUR NAME ABOVE

Instructions to claim your free ebook edition:
1. Visit MorganJamesBOGO.com
2. Sign your name CLEARLY in the space above
3. Complete the form and submit a photo of this entire page
4. You or your friend can download the ebook to your preferred device

ISBN 9781636984025 paperback
ISBN 9781636984032 ebook
Library of Congress Control Number:
2023951883

Cover Design by:
Connor Walden
@connor_walden // www.connorwaldenart.com

Interior Design by:
Christopher Kirk
www.GFSstudio.com

Morgan James PUBLISHING **Builds** with... **Habitat for Humanity®** Peninsula and Greater Williamsburg

Morgan James is a proud partner of Habitat for Humanity Peninsula and Greater Williamsburg. Partners in building since 2006.

Get involved today! Visit: www.morgan-james-publishing.com/giving-back

Contents

In Unison

One day I asked my talented musician wife and parenting partner,[a] Sara, "Why does a composer choose for a choir to sing in unison?"

To clarify, unison singing is singing together, each member singing the same note at the same time, rather than singing in harmony, when members sing different notes that may not be sung at the same time.

Sara promptly answered my question: "To emphasize the text." She explained that the beautiful diversity of harmony can actually detract from the message that the composer is trying to send. Thus, when the composer wants the listener to focus on the message of the text more than the music, the composer chooses unison singing.

As a listener, I find that unison singing can be very powerful. As a parent, I find that unison parenting is equally as powerful. Unison parenting is designed to focus on the message that the parenting partners want to share, while staying on the same sheet of music together, singing the same notes in the same rhythm.

> Unison parenting is designed to focus on the message that the parenting partners want to share, while staying on the same sheet of music together, singing the same notes in the same rhythm.

---

a   Throughout this book, I will refer to parenting partners. I do this to reflect the wide range of parenting situations in modern society, with more than half being single/divorced/remarried situations, grandparents serving as parents, same-sex parenting, and others. I specifically address such situations in the Collective Parenting chapter. This book isn't only for traditional, first-marriage couples but for anyone who is raising or helping raise a child!

I chose the theme of unison parenting for my first parenting book because it may be as important as any idea in parenting. If parents are not on the same page, childrearing becomes fractured.

- Children become confused as to which rules and principles to follow.
- Parents argue more about individual decisions because they do not have a solid framework to begin with.
- A parent who starts to perform badly goes unchecked because there is no agreed standard to which the other parent(s) can point when observing and correcting that parent.
- Children learn how to play the parents to get what they want.
- Ultimately, children have a rougher time growing up and may lack the self-esteem and discipline to be productive adults who make good decisions.

Instead, unison parenting looks more like the image on the book cover. Parenting partners bring their own experiences and opinions, but there becomes a confluence and blending of ideas into a single coherent theme or philosophy that parents share and implement.

The Parenting Context

Let me explain three contexts of this book. The first context is based on three kinds of experience:

- **My own experience raising three now-adult children.** Two boys, Anthony and Austin, were born into our family, and our daughter, Rebecca, was adopted into our family.
- **My experience as a church youth sponsor** for more than thirty years, witnessing the outcomes of thousands of teens and occasionally mentoring their families.
- **Tapping into the experiences of approximately seven hundred families** to whom I have taught parenting classes in my home church over a fifteen-year period.

I suppose the best endorsement of our parenting came from a newly married couple that are friends with our children. This couple told us that Sara and I are their parenting role models because they have closely observed the results of our parenting and they want their future kids to grow up like ours. That's as high of a compliment as a parent can get!

The Christian Context

The second context of this book is the Christian context. You'll find that 80–90 percent of this book is just good parenting sense that would apply to parents of any religion (or lack thereof). There are sections devoted to spiritual development of your child from a Christian perspective.

My viewpoint comes from a lifelong Christian lens. There are assumptions of Christian values and ethics, discipleship that follows Jesus, and a commitment to Christian community found in the church.

There is also a biblical basis, but frankly, the Bible is not organized as a parenting guide per se. The Bible was also written in a different family culture than today. Today's empowerment of women, the idea of two working parents, the flexibility of the definition of *family*, the challenges and temptations for children in modern culture—none of these are specifically defined and addressed in the Bible.

Still, the Bible contains stories and passages that are useful and encouraging for parents. Hence, I have chosen to start each chapter with a Bible verse and a brief meditation that will inform the topic of the chapter.

The Practical Faith Context

Cecil Taylor Ministries' goal is to teach Christians how to live a seven-day practical faith. How do we apply Scripture and our Christian context to real-life problems?

Parenting is full of real-life problems. Practical faith should be a part of our parenting. We're trying to raise disciples who live according to the gospel.

Thus, *Unison Parenting* is a parenting book, a Christian book, and a practical faith book.

What You Can Expect

Unison Parenting is divided into two major sections. The first has to do with parenting fundamentals that apply to all ages, while the second deals specifically with the teen years. Even if your child is young, you'll want to read the **Teen** section and get an idea of where you're heading. I've inserted a fun "intermission" to transition between the sections.

Ideally, you would begin reading this book when your child is in the cradle. That's not going to be the case for 99 percent of you. More likely, I'm addressing you when you're in the middle of parenting your child or children. Thus, I'm asking you to modify your parenting midstream. Whether you're already following my techniques or have taken a different approach, I encourage you to engage the information with an open mind, ready for introspection as I challenge you with new thoughts.

PART ONE:
THE FUNDAMENTALS

Proactive Parenting

Meditation: Proverbs 22:6

"Start children off on the way they should go,
and even when they are old they will not turn from it."

The father was constantly telling the son to be organized. The son seemingly couldn't grasp this idea. He would misplace homework assignments. He would have to search for his car keys before he could leave the house.

One day, the son misplaced his wallet. The father had had enough. "Son, you don't know where your wallet is. Do you know where my wallet is?" The son wasn't sure. The father continued, "There are only three possible places for my wallet: in my pocket, in the end pocket of my gym bag, or on my nightstand. When I come home, I do not take my wallet from my pocket or gym bag until I am standing in front of my nightstand."

The advice didn't seem to take. However, a few years later, after the son had left home and had returned to visit, the father overheard the young man's exasperated phone conversation with his girlfriend. "You don't know where your wallet is? You have to get organized! Do you know where *my* wallet is? There are only three possible places for my wallet..."

The father went to the mother and said, "I can die happy now. My son listened to me and did what I said!"

There are so many times as a parent that you feel like a failure. You feel like your messages aren't sinking in. You feel like you're raising an alien being.

Yet there is hope. That's not to say that you will create a "mini-me" with your child (and that might not even be desirable). But I can assure you, lessons do start to sink in. Life reinforces what you're saying. Kids grow up to become adults and perceive their parents and their wisdom differently.

I can't tell you how often I have clung to Proverbs 22:6 when parenting. According to Proverbs, your job is to train the child. How they receive the training is largely up to them. But if you parent the right way, they will come around eventually. Be encouraged, believe in the proverb's wisdom and fulfillment, and maintain hope that your teaching will stick.

A Proactive Framework

Merriam-Webster defines *proactive* as "acting in anticipation of future problems, needs, or changes."[1] To be proactive parents, you must act in anticipation of what could happen in the future.

Now, you won't be able to anticipate everything. That's why the next chapter is entitled **Reactive Parenting**. But you need to plan for the future as best as possible.

What you need is a framework and the policies that go with it. You might think of the framework as the big picture, and the policies as the details. By creating a framework and policies, you have a model from which to proactively manage your family and your children.

The details of the framework will be unique to your family. I will propose a framework for you to use, but you will customize it for your own personalities, background, family situation, ethnic or national culture, and values.

Your family framework should define what you stand for—what your core values are. I don't think you need to write the Constitution here. As parents, you can agree to a basic list of principles. Be open to modification; you may not think of everything at first. I wouldn't say you want to remove anything important to you, but you might later add qualities or principles you wish you had considered from the beginning.

Just to get you going, here are some keywords and phrases to get you thinking. These are in no particular order, and some of them are not strong values for me, while others are.

- Respect for others
- Valuing beauty and nature
- Priority on family and community
- Importance of church and a spiritual life
- Creativity and curiosity
- Being able to think for yourself
- Belief in and support of traditions and institutions, such as the country and church, or obeying community leaders, such as teachers or police officers
- Love for all; kindness for all
- Be helpful to others; be generous to others
- Fairness and justice
- Developing and maintaining self-control

- Importance of status and success
- Education and the development of knowledge and wisdom
- Loyalty at all costs

Of course, recognize that some of these have to do with your personal qualities, and your child may not possess the same qualities and interests. At the same time, you want to create a culture or context in which the child is brought up. Even if they depart from it as they make their own decisions, you will have provided a clear foundation for them.

Let me share the framework or paradigm in which Sara and I parented. I could probably list ninety things, but these stood out as supreme:

- Develop our children into productive, moral, contributing adults to society and good decision-makers grounded and educated in Christian principles.
- Place Jesus at the center of our family and emphasize that church participation is what we do.
- Treat education seriously since education gives you options.
- Model these qualities as their adult role models.
- Treat each child as an individual with their own gifts and interests.

Here is an example of this last point. Our oldest son, Anthony, played kids baseball and eventually school football. When he was about nine or so, he wanted to try roller hockey. I was against it, mainly because I didn't know anything about it. Also, at his first practice, Anthony could barely stand on his roller blades, while other players whizzed around him. I was afraid he was going to have a bad experience. Yet I let him go forward.

After watching him play his first game, and not too well, I asked Anthony how he liked it. "That's the most fun I've ever had!" he exclaimed. OK, I was on board! Whatever the outcome, I was glad he had found an activity he thoroughly enjoyed, even if I knew little about it and couldn't skate myself.

Though he was never the best skater, Anthony did well enough to eventually make the all-star team as the best defenseman in his league. I'm grateful that he experienced success to pair with the enjoyment that he derived from roller hockey, which he moved on from when he reached middle school.

Frameworks might evolve over time as you and your family change. Let me also show one way in which our framework evolved. When we decided to adopt Rebecca from China, we thought about what message we were sending to our boys. Clearly, as we became an interracial family, we were demonstrating that someone's race didn't matter to us. But we still had to check ourselves. In such an atmosphere, it was possible, even likely, that someday, our boys might bring home a girlfriend of another race (by the way, one did). Were we OK with that possibility? We decided we were, and we were determined that our children would be raised without prejudice as much as possible.

Whatever your framework, let me share one more concept that is a bedrock of everything I will teach and was also a part of our framework for our kids. It's a subset of the first principle in our framework of developing productive, moral adults contributing to society.

To become such an adult, a child needs to develop sound decision-making. We used a model that I will present in the **Adaptive Parenting** chapter for developing decision-making, and I'll talk further about how to grow a teen's decision-making in the **Collaborative Parenting** chapter. For now, I simply want to highlight this principle and encourage you to make it an integral part of your framework because you're going to hear me talk about it **a lot**!

I feel like I need to add one item to everyone's framework: expressions of unconditional love. You're going to hear later in the book about the crippling effect of not expressing love to children. Use all five love languages available.[2]

- Use physical touch, hugging your kids.
- Speak your love aloud regularly. And when they're at their lowest, don't kick them for their mistakes; show them your tender, loving care and support.
- Give them a gift now and then. It doesn't have to be big or expensive. In fact, it's better if it's a gift that demonstrates that you see them and know their preferences.
- Carve out room in your life to spend time with them; as much as possible, make it one-on-one time.
- Serve your children in loving ways—not to coddle them, not to make life easy on them, but as an expression of love. (You'll learn in this book that there's a difference.)

From Framework to Policies

A framework then translates into policies, which govern:

- Behavior of the children.
- Behavior of the family as a whole—how the family interacts together and what each individual's responsibilities and contributions are (including the parents).
- A model for discipline and reward.

Why should you proactively set policy together as parents?

- It is the essence of unison parenting. You want to be united in how the lofty goals of your framework are implemented.
- Policies greatly reduce making up things as you go along.
- You want to achieve consistency in your own parenting behavior.
- You can work out policy details in private, then show unity in front of your children. Policies also help you as parents keep each other in line when one strays, and that can ideally be handled privately as well.

All sorts of examples from our parenting spring to mind. I'll pick just a few to share, the first having to do with the last bullet.

Regarding unity of policy, there was a time as our children got older that Sara felt like they should be able to take on much more in the way of chores. She firmly believed that by sixth grade, each child should do their own laundry. I countered that I thought that was too young, and perhaps ninth grade would be better. We went back and forth on this for a while. I finally relented, not utterly convinced, but willing to get on board.

It's a good thing I was because when the kids saw how firmly Sara was entrenched, they came to me, asking for relief. My message was that this was family policy, I supported it, and they needed to follow the rules. As it turns out, Sara was right: each was quite capable of handling their own laundry in sixth grade, although, of course, there was a learning curve!

Policies helped each of us as parents. Sara tended to be more emotional and was more likely to, say, ground a two-year-old for life than I was! Clearly defined policies for discipline and reward gave her a structure that limited emotional effects.

As for me, I didn't recognize that I was struggling with consistency. A parenting friend pointed out that I was inconsistent, and as a result, I was receiving undesirable child behavior. I realized that when I came home tired from work, I was much more lenient than in other situations because I was too worn out to stick to the policies. Or if I was feeling really good and generous, I might again be lax about the rules. It was teaching our children how to game me to get what they wanted. I had to learn to be consistent and stick to our policies, no matter how I felt that day.

I had to learn to be consistent and stick to our policies, no matter how I felt that day.

There is scientific backing to this idea of consistency in attachment theory. Krista Cantell writes:

When parents are inconsistent in their caregiving, it sends mixed signals to infants about whether or not they can rely on their caregivers to meet their needs. This inconsistency can lead to anxious attachment, which can negatively impact children in the short term and long term . . . During childhood . . . if [parents] told you there could be certain consequences for not following rules, they would only enforce the consequences occasionally. Or maybe your parents would make promises but not come through on them. Although these actions seem minor to us as adults now, they play a strong role in the developing minds of children.[3]

It's impossible for a human to be consistent all the time. But clearly, as parents, we must make consistency a priority. I'll talk more about this in the **Supportive Parenting** chapter.

The Choices Chart—A Model for Compliance, Reward, and Discipline

Let me suggest to you a proven policy for managing your child's behavior. Sara and I used it, and I recommend it highly.

I call it the Choices Chart. I don't take credit for the concept; I read about it in *The Key to Your Child's Heart* by the late Gary Smalley, whose teaching was foundational to our parenting. Smalley himself credited its underlying principles to his family pediatrician, Dr. Charles Shellenberger.

Smalley was a big believer in contracts within the family. I'll talk much more extensively about literal written, signed contracts in the teenager section.

The Choices Chart is a contract of a different sort. It governs the behaviors of everyone in the family. Everyone helps define the contract, and everyone helps govern the contract.

The Choices Chart governs the behaviors of everyone in the family. Everyone helps define the contract, and everyone helps govern the contract.

Let me start by describing how Smalley and his family initiated the idea, then I'll show you how our family did it.

There are three parts to the management of family behavior via contract:

1. Set clearly defined limits by writing a contract.
2. Supervise the living of these limits regularly.
3. Consistently handle resistance through lost privileges.

On their first pass, Smalley's family wrote a lot of verbiage to describe each family limit and what it meant. Then the family decided together what lost privileges each member would have when a limit was violated. Some of the lost privileges were much harsher than the parents would've submitted. (We found the same thing with our kids and watered down the discipline.) Eventually they settled on lost privileges with a twenty-four-hour limit.

Then Smalley's family changed the five limits to start with the letter C. They called their scheme The Five Cs. Those were:

1. **Conforming**: Obey Mom and Dad—not complain, argue, or nag. (Lost privilege: All toys)
2. **Cleaning**: Clean room every morning; clean up after using toys or other items. (Lost privilege: TV)
3. **Chores**: Mow lawn once a week; remove trash every evening; practice piano by 5:30 p.m. (Lost privilege: After-school snack)

4. **Courteous**: Show courtesy at meals, at church, and during outings. (Lost privileges: Joining the family the next time they eat out)
5. **Caring**: Care for people and things. Go to bed on time; brush teeth; be kind to people and things; don't tease, hit, or argue. (Lost privilege: Seeing friends)

The Smalleys would meet for a brief time after dinner to review every child's compliance and assign any lost privileges.[4]

A key point for every family contract situation in the Smalley household was that they used a management proverb, "People do what you inspect, not what you expect."[5] It's an important thought for parents; we tend to set expectations for our children. This method outlines the agreed behaviors, and then parents inspect whether those agreed behaviors were accomplished.

The Taylor Version of the Choices Chart

I should point out that the phrase Choices Chart actually comes from our family; the Smalleys called it Family Limits. We wanted to emphasize that each child was responsible for their decisions, hence the title Choices Chart.

In addition, we felt like a couple of important behaviors that aligned with our family framework had been missed regarding church and schoolwork. So we modified the Choices Chart to contain seven Cs of behavior (notice the Cs in the title and in the behaviors):

1. Chores
2. Cleanliness
3. Courtesy
4. Caring
5. Conforming
6. Classwork
7. Church

Here is the common understanding we developed as a family of what each meant.

1. **Chores**: Everyone had chores. Some were weekly, some were daily, and some rotated (such as who takes out the trash this week). They were assigned in age-appropriate ways since we had a spread of ages. A key message to our children was that in any household in which they might find themselves (family, college roommates, marriage, etc.), there are expectations of every member of the household.

2. **Cleanliness**: This involved several aspects. First, you had to keep your room clean. We tried several ways of inspecting; usually there was a weekly inspection, but we sometimes inspected more frequently. Second, you had to pick up after yourself in common areas—your toys or other possessions couldn't be everywhere, you don't leave your dishes out, etc. Third, as mentioned before, starting in sixth grade, you had to do your own laundry. Cleanliness could, of course, extend to other areas as needed, such as keeping the car clean once driving commenced.

3. **Courtesy**: The expectation was that you would be courteous to others, starting with parents, extending to siblings, and then to others out in the world. Our phrase when they were young was, "If you talk back to us, then you'll talk back to a teacher. If you'll talk back to a teacher, then you'll talk back to a police officer. And if you talk back to a police officer, you'll find yourself in all sorts of trouble!"

4. **Caring**: This had some similarities to the prior two. You had to show you were caring for people and things. For example, if you have an argument with someone, you need to do it in a respectful way. As for things, you respect possessions and don't break them or treat them badly. Caring also was a catch-all for several forms of misbehavior and was applied as needed.

5. **Conforming**: The child was expected to be obedient to parents and to obey immediately. In practice, we gave some leniency for initial balking or reasonable questions. But it only took a couple of stalling tactics or rebellious actions to earn a nonconformance.

6. **Classwork**: Students had to attend class and behave while there. They needed to keep up with their assignments. Passing grades were required, but basically, we pushed them to do as well as they were capable. (If you are only capable of a C, then bring home a C. But if you're capable of an A, then bring home an A.) We tracked their work via the school's online parent portal. Thursday evening was the weekly accounting for progress. It was not the children's favorite night of the week, I can tell you that! Of course, if they were on point, it went smoothly and reasonably.

7. **Church**: Church and Sunday school attendance were mandatory, aside from parental permission for exceptions like a gymnastics meet or visiting another church with a friend. A sleepover was not an excuse. You had to end it early enough to attend; we frequently picked up our child on the way to church. If we hosted a sleepover, parents had to pick up their children fifteen minutes before we left for church or else the child was coming to church with us. (Parents used both options and adapted very well to this rule.) Children were expected to remain in the classroom or sanctuary and to behave while there.

Let me add a side comment on worship attendance. My preacher father believed that a child has to go to church for ten years before they figure out what's going on. So you can start the clock when they're age two, and they'll start to get it at age twelve. Or you can start training them in worship at age twelve, and they'll catch on by age twenty-two. His advice was to start the clock early.

So we did. We were front-row Christians. The kids and I sat in the front row, or close to it, while Sara sang in the choir. Years later, people in our church would tell me how they watched our kids in the front row, watched them behave and watched them grow. Our kids can't say they didn't get exposed to the full worship experience as early as possible!

Back to the Choices Chart: As the children were younger (ranging from late elementary to preschool) when we started the Choices Chart, we parents defined the disciplines. Let me take a moment to note that for preschoolers, you may have to simplify or water down everything even more. The Choices Chart works better as they get into elementary school. But even a preschooler can perform simple chores and can learn to care about others!

For an idea of what chores children are capable of doing at each age, please refer to the **Useful Links and QR Codes** section.

As our children aged and got used to the chart, we revisited the disciplines, and children were included in the discussion of associated discipline. The power of this model is ownership; as Jane Nelson affirms, "Together we will decide on rules for our mutual benefit. We will also decide together on solutions that will be helpful to all concerned when we have problems."[6]

A beautiful result of this participatory system was that there were no arguments over consequences.

A beautiful result of this participatory system was that there were no arguments over consequences. A parent would identify a nonconformance. The child would say, "What's my consequence?" We would say, "I don't know. Go look on the chart and tell me." The child would go to the posted chart in the main hallway and return with the answer. This really defused any emotion over discipline on the part of parent or child.

The only argument, which rarely happened, was whether there was a nonconformance. Occasionally the child would win that argument because we were reasonable parents willing to hear their viewpoint (actually a good quality to develop in your children: to argue for themselves reasonably), but usually they did not win.

I realize there has been some criticism of the reward and punishment model. But I feel that the implementation I've described is a more positive, collaborative way to approach it, especially when you consider the next section.

A Positive Enhancement to the Choices Chart

Over time, we felt like the Choices Chart did not encourage anything beyond the seven Cs. We wanted to instill positive spiritual behaviors without making it a competition, so we came up with something that worked well, based on the fruits of the Spirit.

From Galatians 5:22–23, the fruits of the Spirit are love, joy, peace, patience, kindness, goodness, faithfulness, gentleness, and self-control. The scriptural understanding is that these fruits are cultivated in us by the Holy Spirit and to improve on them means that we are to draw closer to the Spirit, listen to the Spirit, and obey the Spirit.

That's a little much for children to understand, so we simply defined what each meant and encouraged them to follow them. Not only that, but we encouraged them to see the fruits developing in their siblings.

Once a week, usually on Sundays, we would hold a family meeting. Part of the agenda was to review whether anyone had done a great job of exhibiting a fruit of the Spirit during the week. We would also praise and reward exceptional adherence to the seven Cs, such as above-and-beyond caring for another or doing a splendid job with chores. A parent or another child could nominate a child. When we all agreed that the quality had been exhibited, the <u>family</u> got a star on the Choices Chart (not the individual).

Stars were also awarded for As on the report card. Since the family got a star for each A, it was not seen as a competition as much as a contribution.

However, I'm not going to kid you: If you have a C student and an A student in the house, it's going to be difficult for the C student. You might think of alternatives such as B or above or individual targets for each child based on maximizing their own capability.

As the stars accumulated, the children could choose when to cash them in for family outing rewards. For example, ten stars might be going to a favorite fast-food place, thirty stars might be mini golf, and sixty stars might be the amusement park.

As you can see, the Choices Chart was instrumental in:

- Defining and agreeing on acceptable behaviors.
- Inspecting compliance to agreed behaviors.
- Identifying discipline and punishment in advance and without emotion.
- Recognizing demonstration of positive biblical attributes, family values, and educational accomplishments, all vital in our family framework.
- Verbally praising positive behaviors.
- Rewarding the family as a whole for good behavior and celebrating together.

Practical Pointers

The Choices Chart is one implementation of a framework into policies, and I highly recommend it. But there are other ways you can approach the same problem.

What you're ultimately looking for is a consistent framework that adheres to your principles and allows for flexible decisions.

Here are some pointers to keep in mind:

Transitioning to the Choices Chart

When you first introduce the Choices Chart, you may receive some opposition. The children may think this is just a new way for you to be mean. Just like employees that are skeptical when a company asks them to adapt to a new management strategy, children will be skeptical until they see positive change in action.

To try to convince them that you're not simply being mean:

- Start by pointing out advantages such as clarity of expectations and consequences and the possibility for rewards.
- Depending on their age, they may be able to take part in its creation, and that helps give them ownership.
- Be consistent from the outset with your inspection and assignment of consequences. They will start to get the message.

When to Bend Your Own Rules
The rules are the rules, yes, but in some situations, common sense should prevail.

For example, if a child has a school activity that runs late, it may not be reasonable for them to complete all their chores before bed. It's a practical issue of best use of time, not that the child was goofing off. Hence, a parent might make the decision that chores are waived for tonight, or perhaps there is some way to trade chores with another child or to make good later in the week in some fashion.

Safety Concerns
One thing I haven't mentioned is safety. Safety policies must be established and followed, even before the youngsters know what safety means. During our kids' preschool years, for instance, wandering out in the street drew a harsh rebuke and action to imprint that the kid didn't need to be in the street.

From a Choices Chart perspective, safety would fit into the Conforming section because there are rules of the household that must be followed.

As our children grew, we had safety policies when visiting friends or playing outside. Most of these still applied (though perhaps in a different fashion) when they were in high school. Policies included:

- If a gun is visible or accessible, you must return home immediately.
- A parent must be present in the home you are visiting. If not, you are to contact us and/or return home immediately (depending on age, location, etc.)
    - This got extremely difficult to enforce during the teen years. More on that in another chapter.
- When playing outside, you must always be able to see our front porch or back porch, depending on where you were. You are not allowed to run around the neighborhood at will. If there is somewhere else you want to go, return and ask for permission.
- You are allowed to visit a friend, but you do not have the right to go wherever you please while you are out of the house. You're expected to be in that house and nowhere else.

That last point led to a rewarding, humorous moment. Our son Austin was about seven years old, visiting a neighboring family a few houses away. We received a call from the mother, saying that the family wanted to go out for ice cream and take Austin with them, but he refused to budge unless he had permission from his parents. We allowed the trip, thankful that he had followed our rule so precisely.

Building Internal Motivation

As I've said before and will reinforce in the **Adaptive Parenting** and **Collaborative Parenting** chapters, our goal is to produce a functioning adult who makes good decisions. That goal is partially achieved by the child being internally motivated rather than being externally motivated. Put another way, if they are only motivated to perform in order to receive something, the model is not as effective as one where the child assumes responsibility for their motivation.

> If children are only motivated to perform in order to receive something, the model is not as effective as one where the child assumes responsibility for their motivation.

According to the American Psychological Association, there are two ideas to motivate your child. You can emphasize the value of doing the activity while rewarding compliance with positive verbal feedback. You can also assign tasks that are just beyond the child's current abilities.[7] I believe our implementation of the Choices Chart followed these two guidelines.

First, holding the family meeting and recognizing exceptional implementation of the seven Cs and exemplification of the fruits of the Spirit provided positive verbal feedback. As parents, we also tried to thank children as they completed a task. That didn't always happen, but I feel like it happened often enough to be encouraging.

Second, introducing tasks just above children's current abilities reflects how the Choices Chart should evolve as children age. The task of doing laundry in sixth grade is just one example of adjusting their responsibilities, but it's a good one. Believe me, our kids didn't get it right the first time! Perhaps not the second, either. At first, they needed advisory assistance, the ability to ask questions, and permission to experiment without punishment. For example, parents should bite their tongues and give their young launderers some grace on how well or even if they fold clothes after cleaning. After a while, children begin to realize the value of making clothes look nicer once they've made the effort to clean them. But they will likely walk out the door in wrinkled clothes before then!

I know some of you are shaking your heads, but remember, we're trying to instill internal motivation. Experience is sometimes a better teacher than you.

Introducing the Choices Concept to Teens

If you're the parent of a teen, you may already be anticipating the eye rolls over attaching gold stars to a chart. You'll be happy to know that I would suggest something different.

Undoubtedly, if a child grows up with the Choices Chart concept, it is much easier to adapt it as they grow out of the details that work for younger kids. By the way, this adaptation is tricky in a multichild family because of different age ranges, but still possible; four quarters and a dollar bill are very different but equal.[8] You'll have to essentially manage different systems for different children, with some unification on things like contributions toward the rewards program.

In the **Teen** section, I'll offer two age-appropriate techniques: contracts and collaboration. Contracts are a different implementation of the Choices Chart; collaboration is a separate approach for gaining alignment with your teen. But neither means that you are straying from the framework and principles you establish.

If you deconstruct the Choices Chart, the elements are still there that you want to reinforce and utilize:

- Positive behaviors based on family values and rules
- Rewards and bonuses for above-and-beyond good behavior
- Compliance and inspection techniques

When introducing this freshly to a teen, you may want to zero in on their particular issues of rebellion or negative behavior, especially if you have been a parent that has frankly fallen short in the ideal characteristics described in the upcoming **Supportive Parenting** chapter. (You have some remedial parenting to do with yourself if you examine yourself honestly and then truly want to improve your parenting for the sake of your teen.)

For example, if your teen has fallen into a habit of foul language, that may be an area of special attention. While the goal might be to never use foul language, adults understand there are times to never use it and times you might get away with it. So it is partially a moral issue and partially an issue of the fruit of self-control.

Here's a story about converting to a new structure with teens and what not to do.

Sara attended a church retreat where a single mother complained to her about how terrible her middle school children were. They wouldn't do their chores, and they said horrible, disrespectful things to her.

Sara started talking to her about the Choices Chart concept, then suggested she start with the biggest argument they were having: who was to do the laundry. The mother wanted them to be responsible for their own laundry, but the children threw it back on the mom. And she kept accepting that.

We suggested that the mother establish new laundry rules and implement the concept of agreed consequences. In this case, she would not get the buy-in immediately, but she could start with laundry and later expand the rules and the children's participation in the agreement.

The mother did set up the laundry agreement and gained some positive traction on that, despite the grumbling. But she did not follow through with the entire Choices Chart concept, and as a result, she continued having a lot of problems with her children's behavior overall, leading to a ton of bad behavior during the teen years.

Let's park the details of contracts and collaboration until the **Teen** section.

Avoid Manipulation

As I was finishing this chapter, I came across a question to an advice columnist. A mother complained that her children refused to do chores around the house. Readers weighed in, giving parental advice that went completely against what I've presented in this chapter. It ranged from completely giving up hope that the children would comply to making odd threats like, "I'm going to embarrass you by talking to your friends about current events!"

I hope you see the advantage of not making up stuff like that as you go along. Instead, proactively set a course, inspect compliance, and assess agreed consequences. Stick to the plan, execute, and repeat. Parenting doesn't have to use manipulation or smack of desperation.

Laine Lawson Craft writes in her book *The Parent's Battle Plan:*

> *We often feel forced to manipulate our children in ways that are meant to have them act or behave better. The more our children act up or disobey, the more we try to manage and control their actions and bad decisions. This merry-go-round parenting can spiral into an endless stream of push and be pushed. . . . The remedy for my miserable merry-go-round parenting cycle started when I realized that I had never been in control in the first place.*

My manipulation could never produce anything other than losing a battle. I had to give to God any perceived control that I thought I had over my children.[9]

As I'll talk about in the opening meditation of the next chapter, we have a parenting partner in God. We need to realize that our children are in His hands, even if they seem to be slipping from ours. Because of this, we can yield our manipulation and making stuff up as we go along.

Even with God as your partner, you will experience your child's battles and arguments and weaseling and even open defiance at times. But you will eventually see the fruits of your labor, even if it's not at the present moment. (Remember Proverbs 22:6!)

So much of your parenting results show up later. I'm happy to say that when my kids went off to college and became members of new households, they were the ones doing the housework and coaxing others to comply. They knew how to do chores—cleaning the dishes, scrubbing the toilets. They expected other household members to perform their responsibilities. Although they generally complied well growing up, I was still a little surprised to see that they became the organized ones. They revealed themselves as well-functioning adults. So there's hope!

Singing from the Same Sheet of Music

I can suggest principles, frameworks, and policies, but what ultimately drives proactive parenting is the unity of the parents creating and implementing those constructs.

Now that you have information on proactive parenting, and before you go any further, I recommend a serious discussion between parenting partners of what you have read so far. Nothing in this book will work smoothly without buy-in from each parenting partner.

I used a musical analogy in the introduction of this book. Parenting partners have to perform in unison, singing from the same sheet of music, producing the same note at the same time. Wrangle privately together over your proactive parenting measures. Ultimately, just like when my wife and I disagreed on laundry policies, it's critical that you emerge from the room united on the policies, speaking with one voice, backing each other up, remaining consistent, and talking frequently as you go forward about what is working, what isn't, and how to adjust. Because that conversation will happen too—believe me!

You must agree that as parents, you will monitor each other.

In addition, you must agree that as parents, you will monitor each other. There'll be sections in this book that will confront your idea of what a good parent is. You'll need to agree on what good parenting looks like and privately call each other out when the requirement isn't met. This is hard but fair, and it ultimately best serves your child, which is the real goal.

It is impossible to think of everything that could be covered by a parenting policy, and kids will present new circumstances that you never imagined, especially as they get older, and life gets more complicated. You will definitely have to react to situations that your framework does not specifically cover. How do you address those? How do you prevent getting caught off guard? How do you stay vigilant and avoid giving sloppy, ill-thought decisions and responses to your kids? These are the questions addressed in the next chapter, **Reactive Parenting**.

Summary of Proactive Parenting

Key Points

- Establish core values and principles for your family.
- Create policies that match these core values and principles.
- Policies address behavior of the children, behavior of the family as a whole, and the model for discipline and reward.
- The Choices Chart is a recommended way to reflect policies, expectations, consequences, and rewards.
- The Choices Chart will evolve in the teen years to the techniques of contracts and collaboration.
- Setting well-defined expectations and outcomes, then inspecting them regularly, will give consistency, unity, and calm to your family.

Unison Parenting Foundation

- Parents agree on framework and policies.
- Parents work out their differences in private, then publicly unite in implementation and in backing each other up.
- Parents monitor each other to ensure parenting policies and techniques are adhered to, for the sake of the children.

Reactive Parenting

Meditation: Psalm 127:1, 3

"Unless the Lord builds the house,
the builders labor in vain. . .
Children are a heritage from the Lord,
offspring a reward from him."

Is it fair to say there are times when our offspring do not seem like a
reward to us?

One of those times is when they spring something new on us, and it is incumbent on us parents to react to an unforeseen situation.

I laugh at some of the crazy combinations of words that came out of my mouth when our kids were little. I liked a few that I saw in an online article on actual things parents say.[10]

- "Get your spaghetti out of between your toes . . . and keep eating."
- "She is your baby sister, not a pull toy."
- "Why is there a Lego tower in the fridge?"
- "Don't lick the wall. We are in the public bathroom."
- "Why did you paint the couch red!!!?" *(Yes, that one really happened—to a white leather sofa.)*

Some of the unforeseen situations can get complicated and even dangerous. And that's when it's good to zoom out to the big picture.

Remember that the builders labor in vain if the Lord isn't building the house.

We want to raise our children in a Christian home with a firm foundation. Then come the details. As we'll find in later chapters, all sorts of parenting mistakes that were embedded in us by our parents can come tumbling out.

This is why it's best to start with a determination to raise your children in a Christian home with godly principles. That's also why it's best to remember in times of stress and reaction that you have a parenting partner—God!

The one who gave you the offspring also gave you wisdom, character, and love that you can pass on to your children. In the moments when you have to react, when you don't know what to do, God is just a prayer away, just a breath away. Lean on God, as the perfect parent, to guide you, sustain you, and comfort you when life starts to go haywire.

A Reactive Framework

This chapter is partially inspired by the worst parenting mistake I ever made. I'm not going to tell you all the details, primarily to spare the child who was involved. The details of my poor parenting will come out later in this chapter. But I'll start by saying that I didn't react in the proper way to a new situation, and you'll be the better for my mistake!

First, let me address that the term *reactive parenting* is toxic in most parenting books. I agree when the term is used synonymously with *knee-jerk reaction*. It can mean not having a plan. It can mean yelling instead of thoughtfully disciplining. But that is not how I'm using the term *reactive parenting*.

I define *reactive parenting* as "reaction to new situations outside the planned proactive framework." By this definition, reactive parenting is a positive and necessary option.

> I define *reactive parenting* as "reaction to new situations outside the planned proactive framework." By this definition, reactive parenting is a positive and necessary option.

The problem I'm addressing in this chapter is that you can't plan for everything; sometimes you have to react to new situations. You can try to plan. You can strategize. You can prepare. You can drill. Thank God that when Buffalo Bills safety Damar Hamlin suffered a cardiac arrest during an NFL game in Cincinnati, the team's medical personnel, the stadium personnel, NFL medical personnel, and the nearby hospital all had a plan in place that they had practiced for just such an emergency.

On the other hand, preparations don't mean that something won't go wrong when the actual situation occurs. When I was working in high tech, I recall laughing at this mass email I received from the building manager while I was traveling:

Thank you to everyone who participated in today's tornado drill. Unfortunately, everyone committed what would have been a seri-

ous error in case of an actual tornado. Remember that a whistle indicates a tornado is occurring, while an alarm means a fire is occurring. Please do not march outside into a tornado when you hear the whistle!

You can plan and plan, but your kids will find ways to create new, unexpected situations to which you must react. So what do you do?

I'll give you three keywords: **identify, question,** and **communicate**.

Identify, Question, and Communicate

Hopefully, as a parent, you will develop a "spider-sense," where you get that tingling when something is wrong or different. (I have a story about that later in the chapter, in the section on **Assigning Consequences in New Situations**.) It's really important to get a sense of when something is off, wrong, or unusual, and identify that it is out of the norm.

For example, say your child asks if they can go to a concert with a friend. Perhaps this is the first time they've made such a request. Thus, it's new to them, and depending on your parenting experience, it may be new to you. You begin by **identifying** that this is a request requiring close attention. So you drop what you are doing so you can provide that close attention (or delay the discussion until you can pay attention).

Second, you need to **ask questions**, such as:

- What is the topic of the concert, or who is performing?
- Where is the concert?
- Who is going with you?
- How will you get there?
- Who is driving?
- What adult is supervising this adventure?
- How can I get in touch with that adult if something goes wrong?
- What time does the concert start, and when is it expected to end? (Curfew discussion follows.)
- Etc., etc., etc.

My kids came to know that it was much better to anticipate questions and have the answers ready or else they would just have to go away to research them. I was like that old Geico commercial with former NBA player Dikembe Mutombo swatting away paper wads as he coursed through an office, wagging his finger and saying, "No—no—no!" I would just swat away the questions that had poor answers: "Don't bring that weak stuff in here!"

By the way, there is a lot of long-term value in your kids understanding the drill for providing answers to questions. In future school settings and in future jobs, they will have the basis for thinking through things more deeply, anticipating questions from superiors or peers, and having well-considered answers ready.

This questioning will likely frustrate the kids, as they might have to go away to research two or three times, partly because the answers weren't satisfactory, partly because the parenting partners thought of new questions.

In the midst of this, it's important to **communicate** with your parenting partner. Let them know that you have **identified** a new situation, that you are in the midst of **asking questions**, and you are **communicating** the situation to them. Ask them if they have questions as well. Depending on where everyone is located (your parenting partner may not be readily available), you could invite them into the conversation or handle it yourself, still clearly and rapidly communicating with your parenting partner.

Let's take another situation. Perhaps your child has gone to several concerts before with friends and parent chaperones. But something about a new concert request seems different. Again, the questions will help, but you may have to drill down for other information.

Perhaps the group is using a driver you don't know. Perhaps you've assumed the concert is in your city, but this one is in a city an hour away. Perhaps they're suggesting a concert plus a sleepover since they'll be getting home so late this time. That last statement should cause a big "Hmm" in your mind, as you begin thinking through situations, like what shape they'll be in when they leave the concert. Is this a cover to use drugs or alcohol without you finding out?

In this case, you should be **identifying** that this is not the usual concert request. Of course, this will bring more probing **questions**. And of the utmost importance, you'll be **communicating** with your parenting partner to gain their feedback.

I'm tempted to say that communication is the most important element of Identify, Question, Communicate, but all three steps are equally important.

I'm tempted to say that communication is the most important element of the three, but all three steps are equally important. For example, if you haven't identified that this concert request is different, you may not ask proper questions, and you may communicate incorrect information to your partner. It's one thing to communicate, but it's another to communicate insufficiently.

Now let's look at specific scenarios where reactive parenting comes in handy.

Fighting Divide-and-Conquer

This is probably the first situation you'll encounter with your child because they figure out this tactic at a young age. I call it Divide-and-Conquer, and it works like this:

- Make a request to parent 1
- Receive a *no*
- Make the same request to parent 2
- Receive a *yes*

It's not unusual for one parent to give a different answer than the other. It isn't necessarily that the parents aren't **in agreement** but that they are not **in unison**. Often, one parent might have some information that the other parent doesn't have.

This can cause the No parent to get angry with the Yes parent. I would say it's important to keep the temperature low between you because what has really happened are two things:

- Your child has gamed you.
- Neither of you adequately communicated with the other. So, both parents are at fault.

Classic example: "Can I go to so-and-so's house?"

Maybe in normal cases, this would draw a routine "OK," and a parent would give permission. But the other parent might know something, such as the child has a lot of homework, there's a conflict on the schedule, or the child was just grounded for some reason.

Let me pronounce this edict: **"Woe unto the child who plays Divide-and-Conquer!"**

If you think about it, this is potentially a violation of multiple items on the Choices Chart:

- **Conformance**: Remember how they are to accept a parent's instruction immediately?
- **Caring** or **Courtesy**: The child is showing disrespect to the parent in not accepting the answer and manipulating the situation to get the answer they want.
- **Classwork** or **Chores**: Depending on the situation, they may be skirting their duties on homework or chores.

From the parenting perspective, you're not always going to have the same information or the opportunity to tell each other. What can you do to react to this situation?

- **More sharing of information**. Parenting partners need to be communicating throughout the day. Say that one parent is at work; a text message is likely sufficient: "FYI, I've told our daughter that she can't go out to play until all homework is done."
- **More questions**, especially if you have gained that parenting spider sense: "Have you asked your mother already if you can have a snack?"
- **Make a new policy afterward** if one seems required.
- **Consider other situations** similar to this one and set policy.
- **Best: Train the child not to game you**. With consistent enforcement of consequences, they will learn to stop playing this game.

Giving Permission in New Situations

I have already written about this topic in the **Identify, Question, and Communicate** section, but now I want to discuss what **not** to do to give permission in new situations. I must point the finger at myself because this was my biggest parenting mistake: not communicating.

Without getting into every detail, during their teen years, one of our children approached me with a rather unusual request. I wasn't sure what to make of it. It was outside the bounds of anything they had ever requested. It also seemed to have something mysterious behind it. I correctly **identified** it as a new situation.

I asked **questions**. Why did this request come about? What was behind it? If I said yes, what would happen then?

I did finally say yes, but I also assigned some limitations on the yes and how it would be handled.

But I didn't say anything to my wife. I didn't communicate.

But I didn't say anything to my wife. I didn't **communicate**.

This was a huge mistake to begin with. In fact, I made several mistakes.

- I should have, at minimum, let her know this was going on.
- I was confused enough by the request that I should have gotten a second opinion.
- I should have asked if she had any questions.
- I should have gained her agreement on the answer.

I did none of these. In retrospect, we agreed that she would have quickly vetoed this request.

Instead, the child and I went forward, and a couple of things went dreadfully wrong, endangering my child in a number of ways.

As it turned out, the child was not completely forthcoming about the reasons for the request. Even though I asked the question, I did not have the correct information. My parenting spider sense went off, but I turned off its alarm too quickly. If I had been told the complete story, not only would I have denied the request, but there are other actions I would have taken to address the situation.

Second, the child went outside our agreed limitations, which put them in danger.

It wasn't a great moment for them, and it wasn't a great moment for me. The ramifications impacted them for many months.

All I can say is, Identify, question, and communicate. Don't get sloppy or lazy. Remain vigilant. Stay on target.

Assigning Consequences in New Situations

Sometimes a new situation warrants new consequences that go beyond the Choices Chart or its teenager replacement. Perhaps the situation involves multiple violations. Perhaps it breaks a rule that isn't clearly called out contractually but is also clearly very wrong.

Here's a case study of a family that experienced that situation and what they did.

Their daughter (I'll call her Brie) was usually very reliable. She was the type of personality who was straitlaced and would do what she was supposed to do. If Brie said she was at a particular place, a parent could be sure that she was there.

One day Brie texted both parents to say that she and her best friend would be studying at the high school after classes were done. Both parents agreed.

But driving home from work, the father's spider-sense kicked in. He decided to drive past the high school. Although a lot of cars were still in the parking lot because of after-school activities, his daughter's car was not one of them.

He called Brie to ask where she was.

"I'm at the high school," she replied.

He said, "Well, I'm in the parking lot, and your car's not here. So where are you?"

Brie then confessed that her best friend had talked her into going to a nail salon instead of studying. The father told Brie to take her friend home and return home as soon as possible.

Meanwhile, the father called the mother at home and let her know what had happened. They agreed to discuss the situation further when he arrived home.

From the perspective of Brie's parents, there were all sorts of breaches of trust involving both girls:

- A lack of obedience to the family rules (using the Choices Chart nomenclature, this would be a Conforming violation).
- Not studying when expected (Classwork).

- Lying to the parents (per the **Proactive Parenting** chapter, this could be considered Caring or an issue of the fruits of the Spirit).
- Not being reliable to the other girl's parents. They basically would say yes to their daughter for any activity, providing Brie was there; they trusted Brie completely, and now that trust was broken.
- As for the best friend who wanted her nails done, she was aware of Brie's family's rules but tempted Brie to violate them anyway. This breached trust with Brie's parents.

Brie's family had no policy that would cover all these violations at once. They didn't want to cobble existing rules and consequences together, yet they wanted to clearly address this particular situation. So, when their daughter arrived home, the parents wisely told Brie that they would discuss the consequences and sent her off to her room.

Later, they called an apologetic Brie to join them and accepted her apology. But they also assigned consequences and new rules that had to be adhered to for Brie to regain their trust. Among several were these:

- Brie was not allowed to drive anyone for a month.
- Moreover, after that month, she was not allowed to drive her best friend until the friend apologized to Brie's parents for leading their daughter astray.
- Upon request, Brie was supposed to send her parents a Snapchat of where she was at the moment. (In those days, Snapchat photos could not be stored and sent later, so you had to share an immediate photo.)

To her credit, Brie actually suggested the details on that last item, as the parents asked her for ideas for a credible way of knowing where she was at any time.[b]

The parents also offered a path to how Brie could regain trust and remove the consequences.

---

b   Of course, there is technology that will track cars and humans. I will explain in the Teen section why I don't recommend using such technology as a control tool to track your teen's whereabouts, with certain exceptions.

To the parents' credit, they got several things right in their reactive parenting to assign consequences in a new situation.

- First, **they quickly got in unison.** The father called the mother with the update, and they huddled once he was home.
- **They did not let their anger get the best of them.** Despite their frustration and disappointment, they were calm and reasoned in their approach to handling this particular situation. They could have easily reacted without thinking or even agreeing (the father could have started angrily assigning consequences to Brie from his car phone).
- **They created natural consequences** instead of just a general grounding or assigning consequences that had nothing to do with this situation.
- **They made the girls understand how they had hurt others by the girls' actions.** The girls had been given a lot of leeway and responsibility, and they had abused it. As a result, they had to earn back trust.

Most situations will not require inventing new consequences, especially when your children are preteens. Your tools of Choices Chart, contracts, and collaboration will typically be enough. But in reactive parenting, you are able to realize when the landscape has changed, when the tools do not fit, and when custom solutions are needed.

Huddle Now

When I have taught this concept in parenting classes, this is the point where I ask parenting partners to take a few minutes to review these reactive scenarios. I ask them to consider two questions:

1. Which of these scenarios have you already encountered?
2. What new ideas did you get from these scenarios?

I suggest you huddle now (or soon) to consider these questions as well. The first will naturally cause you to think about how you handled such situations in the past—what you did right, what you would do differently now. The second will hopefully not only reveal new ways of handling the situations but also lead you to think of additional reactive scenarios that go beyond the ones identified in these pages.

The underlying similarity between proactive and reactive parenting is that we are trying to shape, monitor, approve, and critique the child's decisions. Ideally, we want them to make good decisions. How do we create an environment that teaches good decision-making? That's the topic of the next chapter on **Adaptive Parenting**.

Summary of Reactive Parenting

Key Points

- When faced with an unexpected situation:
  - **Identify** that this is an abnormal case.
  - **Ask questions** to understand the situation thoroughly.
  - **Communicate** quickly and extensively with your parenting partner.
- The child's Divide-and-Conquer technique may work if the parents aren't in unison, even if they're in agreement.
- The repercussions of making a mistake when giving permission in new situations can impact or even endanger your child.
- Take your time when assigning consequences in new situations. Ideally, slow down and decide in unison with your parenting partner.

Unison Parenting Foundation

- Following the process of Identify, Question, Communicate allows you to stay in unison with your parenting partner in unforeseen situations.
- It is easy to get sloppy and miss a step in Identify, Question, Communicate, with potentially dire ramifications. Hold yourself and your parenting partner accountable to follow the process.

Adaptive Parenting

Meditation: Proverbs 3:12

"Because the Lord disciplines those he loves,
as a father the son he delights in."

How does a child learn how to ride a bicycle?

It typically starts with someone who knows how to ride a bike, such as a parent, helping them sit on the bike while steadying them.

Then the helper instructs them to pedal and runs along behind the bike, steadying them and picking them up when they inevitably fall.

This process continues until the parent cannot keep up with the more steady, more confident cyclist, who then dashes off on their own.

Oh, sure, the child hasn't mastered everything. They may take a tumble. They may run into trash cans or a light pole. But they learn, and they learn well. Right? Later in life, we say, "It's like riding a bicycle." You retain the lesson.

Wouldn't parenting be easier if we naturally assumed that the pattern of the bicycle repeats itself hundreds of times with every new technique, every new situation, every new age the child encounters? We can't ride the bike for the child, no more than we can (or should) make every decision for them.

Inevitably, their decisions will fail, and there will be consequences, perhaps worse than skinning a knee. The ideal parent will correct. The ideal parent will pick them up. The ideal parent will lovingly send them off to their next adventurous decision, just as the Lord corrects us even as He loves us deeply.

Adapting to Keep Up with Your Child

One of the most complex, and also emotional, parts of parenting is watching your child change.

Yes, you feel joy in seeing them age and grow. At the same time, it's hard to see your little one become a bigger one and so forth until they are out the door.

In this chapter, I want to discuss ideas on how to adapt our parenting as children age, as well as how to adapt our own feelings.

It starts with conquering our own fear.

- Fear of the unknown.
- Fear of change.
- Fear of losing control.
- Fear of one era slipping away into another era.

- Fear of the new person in your midst.

While adults tend to change slowly, children change rapidly. This is where we get the idea that they are "monsters."

- That last fear is absolutely a fear. While adults tend to change slowly, children change rapidly. This is where we get the idea that they are "monsters," as some parents will put it. In my experience and in my view, it's because the parent is not adapting fast enough to where the child is today.

It is easy to pigeonhole a child and think you have them figured out. You convince yourself that a child is a certain way, then you mentally defend that view even when the evidence is changing. It's vital to freshen your view of your child and keep up with what they are becoming. Sometimes their evolution is more drastic than you might think or expect.

I recall a middle schooler in my church youth group whom I'll call Harry. Harry was typically standoffish and quiet. He came from a single parent home. He would literally go stand in the corner, away from others. Harry didn't want to be touched; if someone went to put their arm around him or even shake his hand, he would pull away.

One Sunday evening, Harry showed up and was suddenly hugging all the girls in the group. Did I take it that Harry was sexually driven or a creep? No! I took it that it was time to meet the new Harry. Harry had changed. The hugging was a sign of a new person. And indeed, talking to Harry that evening, it was like talking to a different person.

I teach parents to reintroduce themselves to their child every six months (if not more frequently). The old child is gone; the new one is here, and only for a while. Of course, if you observe a sudden change as I described with Harry, you need to accelerate that reintroduction.

This reintroduction process starts earlier than you might think. For example, you see it as your child turns from infant to toddler. Yes, welcome to the

Terrible Twos! Well, in my parenting case, the tantrums didn't happen so much until three years old, but nonetheless, it's an era when suddenly you're dealing with a different child than before. It takes some understanding of their age and stage and perspective to deal with such changes.

For example, in the case of toddler tantrums, *Washington Post* advice columnist Carolyn Hax stated the situation very well as a communication issue, one that would return over time:

> *Tantrums are generally misunderstandings that toddlers don't have the skills to clear up the usual way . . . File all this away for adolescence, when children's emotional range once again grows faster than their communication skills do.*[11]

The reason this is a problem in adolescence is that your teen is rapidly learning words (seven to ten per day), but their emotional need is greater in terms of friendships, romantic and sexual desires, engagement with the wider world, desire and fear of the future, and more. Their vocabulary and communication skills, especially in the early teen years before driving age, can trail their emotional needs.

Understanding where children are today in their progression, especially in communication skills, is essential. This book is not designed to dive deeply into developmental progression. Please refer to the **Useful Links and QR Codes** section for resources that can get you started on this complex, wide-ranging topic.

Returning to the topic of your child's evolution, you'll also hear yourself saying things like, "You liked this food before. Why don't you like it now?" Simple things like taste bud changes happen. Hey, at the cellular level, those cells are swapping quickly! Your child is literally becoming a new person constantly.

The brain develops rapidly but not evenly. By age five, your child's brain is already 90 percent of the size of an adult brain.[12] But the prefrontal cortex, where critical thinking and decision-making takes place, does not fully build out until the mid-twenties.[13] (Sarcastically, we parents could add, "If then!")

I used to say that I was scared to play pickup games of basketball or football with older teenagers in our church youth group because they had most of their physical prowess but not the decision-making to go with it—which explains why during a pickup basketball game, a 250-pound football player got mad at me for playing better than him and trucked me, one hundred pounds lighter, into the basketball standard! (Luckily, I saw him coming and curled up into something like a fetal position right before he slammed into me.)

A Unison View of Every Age

Before I move on, I want to emphasize how important parental communication is regarding how the child is growing and how the parents must adapt.

It's hard to remember an exact example, but my wife Sara was excellent at telling me about the events of the day while I was at work or traveling and how our children were changing. She had a heightened sense of their growth.

Paired with my view of reintroducing yourself to your child, I felt like we were able to keep pace with change and pivot quickly to the new people populating our house.

Hence, I would put you and your parenting partner(s) on alert for change in the child. Be watchful and mindful of behavioral changes.

- Perhaps the change is how the child reacts to a situation differently than before.
- Perhaps it's a change of habits.
- Perhaps it's a change of attitude.
- Perhaps it's an emotional change that is revealing itself.

There was a family whose daughter was in competitive sports. The parents had one particular view of their daughter, "Olivia." But in comparing notes with the girl's coaches, the parents realized she had changed in the competitive environment. They saw Olivia as even-keeled, while the coaches saw her as emotional. Her parents saw Olivia as enjoying the sport, while the coaches saw her as stressed out by the sport. This led to the parents updating their view and having conversations with the daughter to understand her perspective. As it so happened, what was once a pleasurable sport had become more of a burden to Olivia as the competition increased.

To round out this idea, remember that our goal is unison parenting. We want to have the same viewpoint. Communication is important. Evaluation is important; was this incident today with the child a sea change, or was it a simple anomaly? Planning to watch and evaluate going forward is essential. And once it's agreed that the child is a new person, the parents should discuss how to respond to the change and what it means to their parenting going forward.

> Adaptive parenting is difficult because parents need to agree and to see the same way.

Don't underestimate the potential conflict. Adaptive parenting is difficult because parents need to agree and to see the same way. It's not unusual for one parent to be atop the change, while the other is dismissive. Sometimes you can't agree right away, so you instead need to agree how you will monitor the child and when you will again discuss your views.

I started this chapter by talking about decision-making and want to return to that topic now as one of the essential aspects of adaptive parenting.

The Dilemma of Freedom vs. Control

There's an old saying that bad decisions lead to bad experiences, which lead to good decisions that lead to good experiences.

I just spent a good portion of the last chapter saying that your child can experience dire ramifications when you give your permission to a bad decision. Now in this chapter, I'm going to tell you to let them make decisions.

Actually, it won't be that simple. I'll describe how to adapt your parenting to grow your child's decision-making, how to override bad decisions while allowing them to gradually take more control, how to limit those bad decisions and bad experiences (or at least their impact), leading to good decisions as a result of the experience.

Here's a funny example of allowing a decision with limited consequences. A few months after we adopted our daughter from China, we held my birthday celebration. It was the first time Rebecca had ever seen a birthday cake. It was the first time she had seen candles. Actually, since we were celebrating my forty-fourth birthday, the candles were numeral candles, each in the shape of a four.

Rebecca was completely fascinated by the candles. I'm not sure if, as she was learning English, she confused the word *candles* with *candy*. Regardless, she wanted to eat the candles!

I spent at least five minutes trying to explain to my second-language three-year-old that she must not eat the candles. Then I made a great parenting choice: I let her make the decision.

With a napkin ready, I said, "OK, you can eat the candles!" Rebecca grabbed one and took a bite. Her nose turned upward, and her face scrunched as she chewed the wax. Then I held out the napkin and said, "Now spit it out." And she gratefully spit the contents into the napkin.

My sister was present and thought I was a horrible parent for letting her eat the candle. I said, "I could have spent all evening arguing with her over eating the candle. It only took five seconds for her to experience and understand what I was saying."

I considered it fantastic parenting. I let my child make a decision I knew was wrong. I was able to limit and manage the consequence.

I considered it fantastic parenting. I let my child make a decision I knew was wrong. I was able to limit and manage the consequence. She had a bad experience, and she learned from it. She never tried again to eat a candle!

Ultimately, we want our children to gradually learn how to make good decisions. In this chapter, I will suggest a process for growing their decision-making capability in age-appropriate ways.

In the long run, in the teen years, the decisions will get more complex and so will the parenting model for growing decision-making. I'll present this advanced structure in the chapter **Collaborative Parenting**.

Incremental Decision-Making

I want to show you the adaptive parenting model for decision-making that Sara and I used. I don't recall getting this out of a book or another source. It was something we created, but most likely, it was influenced by both experience and by reading.

I call it incremental decision-making. It's a structure to incrementally allow them more latitude in making decisions. The model is tied to age and stage, but obviously, you will experience variations within it for the specific pace at which your child is maturing and making decisions.

A unison parenting point is that you and your parenting partner should agree on adopting this model of adaptive parenting. It will not work without agreement on how to grow your child's decision-making. In addition, it's important to work together to understand how your child's decision-making is progressing, to identify when to move to another stage, and to align on important principles such as letting your child fail.

The model is divided into three broad age ranges.

- Ages zero to six
- Ages six to twelve
- Ages twelve to eighteen

Let me show you the overview, then I'll dive into details and how to implement it, so that you are gradually bringing your child to a point of making good decisions on their own.

Ages Zero to Six

Incremental
Decision-Making

Age	Child's Decision-Making Scope	Managing Consequence	Parental Explanation
0-6	**Small, limited.** Typically Parent. A or B decisions.	Allow low consequence decisions.	None
6-12	**Slightly larger, grows by age 10.** Parent decides, often with child's input. Child's decisions are routine, low scope, low consequence. Child makes more sophisticated A-B-C decisions with some trade-off analysis.	Protect against big consequences. Allow lower consequences to happen.	Explain the concept of incremental decision-making and how they will gradually get to make more decisions as they approach age 12.
12-18	**Much wider, but under parental control where possible.** Child eventually makes decisions in your absence. Work as partners in other decisions. Parent retains consultant role and veto power.	Be clear on consequences. Try to limit consequences and prevent worse-case scenarios. Guide child to understand and articulate variety of options.	*Explain collaborative approach (later in book).* Focus on the prize, namely, independent decision-making as the goal at key milestones: • Driving – new responsibilities and consequences. • Post-High School – future life options and decisions.

The simple way to put this is that you make all decisions for the child. Of course, we know it's more complicated than that. A child wants to assert independence very early on, and it's important to allow them some freedom.

So while the child won't decide on their own on a topic like what preschool they will attend, they can decide what to wear today.

Usually the best way to do that is to narrow their choices, then let them decide. For example, two choices: A or B. You can take other choices off the table: "That's not a choice." In some situations, you can be open to a child's creativity on decisions.

Bad decisions should have low consequence and help learning. For example, the child generally can't make decisions that risk an injury any worse than an owie. Some bad decisions may mean that a mess results; determine your own comfort level with messes and let those happen.

I remember a time when I briefly left our two preschool boys to their own designs. It happened at church on an Easter Sunday. Sara was singing in the choir, and I was sitting in one of the front rows with the boys. The congregation was invited to come into the choir loft to sing the "Hallelujah Chorus." This is something I always enjoyed, and I wanted to do it. So I told the boys to be good for five minutes while I went up to sing. What could go wrong? They were right there where I could see them.

Well, my focus was not so much on my children except to know that they were still there, behind some standing adults in prior rows. I could tell they were very involved with something, but that's it. When I returned from singing, the boys proudly showed me what they had been doing: decorating each other's faces with Sharpies!

After some research on Sharpie removal and plenty of washing (Sara says, "Lots of scrubbing. LOTS of scrubbing!"), the boys were clean again and had learned a lesson from their decision. They never made that mistake again! (Nor did I, for that matter!)

Ages Six to Twelve

The next adaptation to your parenting is that the child can gradually begin to make decisions within a structure, where you evaluate alternatives together, discuss pros and cons at times, narrow the options to something like A–B–C, and allow the child to choose.

> The next adaptation to your parenting is that the child can gradually begin to make decisions within a structure.

You're still providing a pretty stout safety net to protect against consequences of decisions, and you retain veto power. But you can pick your spots to let a bit more consequence happen.

By the way, it's OK and even necessary for your child to fail now and then, from the beginning, but especially during this phase. Failure and struggle are truly a part of life. In the long run, you want to create a resilient person who can handle inevitable failure and can overcome struggles to become proficient or to achieve a goal. Don't protect them so much that they can't make a mistake.

A classic example comes in managing sleepovers. Especially as they reach upper elementary, sleepover invitations arrive. If your child is active in extracurriculars, it may mean that the sleepover is the night before a game in which they're playing.

The conversation typically goes like this:

Mom: *If you go to this sleepover, you may not be rested for the game. You may be tired and not perform well.*

Kid: *Oh, come on, Mom! I'll be fine. I'll be able to play the game, and I can take a nap afterward if I'm tired.*

If you agree to let them try, they will soon find out exactly how dragged out it makes them feel to go to bed well after normal bedtime but then perform the next day. I'll tell you, this is like the candle/candy story; there is no greater teacher than letting them try and experience the consequences.

Now, if it's the championship game, you might want to protect the child (and their coach) with a firm "not this time." But in other cases, I say let them make the decision.

This situation also leads to exploring alternatives. For example, an alternative is to go to the sleepover but leave at 9 p.m. ("Aw, Dad, can you make it 10?") You can offer to bring them home for a controlled finish to the day so they can prepare well for tomorrow.

You'll be surprised at how much they remember how they felt when operating on inadequate sleep. In my parental experience, children will often make the more conservative decision in ensuing opportunities.

At this age, you can also start teaching them how to analyze a situation and weigh alternatives. A great example in our family was mobile phone ownership.

In my opinion, kids receive cell phones way too early. They are very expensive play toys that carry a lot of risk in various ways.

In my view, a child doesn't need a mobile phone until they are of an age to be somewhere unsupervised, where they need to be able to call their parents if needed (e.g., after an extracurricular activity). It wasn't very persuasive to me that other kids owned mobile phones. (A mother from my parenting classes wrote me, "Your lessons helped us realize that it was ok to say 'no' when other parents would say 'yes' or 'they are just being teens.' ")

Our family policy was that we would purchase a cell phone for the child when they began driving. However, the child was allowed to purchase their own cell phone and pay their share of service on the family plan anytime from sixth grade onward.

I used a spreadsheet with our children to calculate the cost of a mobile phone. Their sources of money at a young age included gifts, allowances, and paid chores. We estimated how much money they spent on things like candy or video games. Then they could see the impact of a mobile phone. Every one of my children decided to delay the purchase of a cell phone until later; as I recall, they all waited until eighth grade.[c]

One thing that is important to start doing during this age window, especially upper elementary, is to let them in on your plan for incremental decision-making. There are a few points you can make clear to gain better buy-in and begin partnering together on decision-making. Here is a script, but you can modify it as you feel comfortable with your child and your family values in mind.

- "We are growing your decision-making. We want you to start making decisions so you're good at it when you get older."
- "However, we parents still retain the right to overrule your decision if we think it's unsafe or unwise. We'll explain to you why we're saying no and will work on other choices with you."
- "As you get into middle school and high school, you'll gradually make more and more decisions. Just think: When you start driving, you'll make a lot of very important decisions while driving that can impact other drivers and people in your car. So we definitely want you to become a good, mature decision-maker."

---

c   This same spreadsheet was used to calculate the cost of smoking, which illustrated how it would harm their finances if they took up smoking. It was a deterrent.

It's good to remind them of this policy from time to time (yeah, they'll forget it), continuing up until the time they are prepared to leave home.

Ages Twelve to Eighteen

In the second half of the book, I'll have much more to say about both how to teach and encourage decision-making in your teen, and how to manage their choices during those years. For now, let me amplify what is in the **Incremental Decision-Making** chart from above.

In the teen years, it's essential to teach your child decision-making skills because the truth is that your child will begin deciding things without you around.

- They will find themselves in social settings without you.
- They will encounter more complex scenarios at school without you.
- They will run into interpersonal complexities without you.
- They will find themselves behind the wheel of a car without you.
- And they simply won't share a lot of situations with you, either to hide the situation from you or because it may not occur to them that you should be aware or consulted.

If you can adapt your parenting to establish a partnership with your child, you'll find yourself involved as a consultant and escalation point. For example, there was a girl, "Kelsey," who became the president of a club in her high school. Power struggles and interpersonal difficulties arose. Because she had never faced something like this but her parents had established a trusting relationship, she was able to consult her parents on ideas and options for addressing those issues. Eventually Kelsey decided to leave the club altogether—perhaps not the ideal situation, but it was the best decision for her own stress level and emotional well-being.

Sometimes, their choices have bigger ramifications. A fellow father shared that his son, "Brayden," suddenly was headed out the door after curfew. The dad, naturally, asked what he was doing. Brayden explained that his friend, a girl, had called from a party and asked him to come get her. The boy she had come to the party with was too drunk to drive, and the party was getting too wild for her comfort.

The dad encouraged his son to hustle over. Brayden entered the party, found the girl, and headed out. Suddenly multiple police cars arrived to break up the party and arrest teens for underage drinking. The first people they encountered were Brayden and his friend. The police determined fairly quickly that neither had been drinking and told them to get away from the party immediately, which they gratefully did. The party was put to an end, and a number of people got to learn what it's like to ride in the back of a police car!

While it was a close call, both Brayden and his friend made good decisions to get out of a bad situation. I would assert that good parenting helped both of them make good decisions at a critical time.

One of the keys to partnering with your teen is to convince them that your mission is not control but protection. You realize that they are going to make decisions without you. Therefore, you want to prepare them, you want them to consult with you, and you are still going to provide guardrails. There will be limits on what they can do. There will still be rules to follow and consequences to pay for misalignment. But because life is going to start giving them big consequences for bad decisions, your goals are to protect them while they learn about adult-level decision-making and to prepare them for the day when they will stand on their own.

This will be a tougher sell for some kids than others. But you'll notice something interesting: As they approach bigger and bigger decisions, they get more scared. They start to realize the magnitude of wrong decisions. They may become indecisive (a trait you'll want to help them overcome). They may even go so far as to ask you to tell them what to do. And then comes the rich moment when you tell them, "I'm going to help you, but it's your decision to make."

Let me pivot now to addressing some traps you may fall into, if not careful.

Your Child Does Not Come with a Remote Control

Some of us are wired to grab control when things go haywire. Some of us just like to be controlling in many situations. It's tempting to try to fully control your child, as if you're controlling a character in a parenting game, and make sure their behavior always aligns with your expectations. I advise against this.

I recall reading a story by a football recruiting expert who witnessed a Rising Senior Day at a major university's football program. He mentioned one soon-to-be high school senior who visited with his mother. This mother was very controlling of everything surrounding her son and spoke on his behalf. The writer quipped, "She treated him like a five-year-old at an alligator farm."

This is the opposite of what I've been preaching. I don't believe the principles I've shared and will share will produce a seventeen-year-old that needs to be treated like a five-year-old. Your goal is to raise your child into an adult who can make great decisions on their own. Clearly, this young man was not on such a path. This kind of control, as we'll learn in the next chapter, can produce rebellion and worse decisions when the fledgling adult begins to make them on their own.

Don't think of your child as a creature with a joystick that you need to operate in order to get the behavior you want.

Your Child Is Not a Mirror

One of many reasons for controlling a child is because of how we feel their behavior reflects on our parenting. Few parents are able to escape this feeling, but mature parents can control the feeling.

> One of many reasons for controlling a child is because of how we feel their behavior reflects on our parenting. Few parents are able to escape this feeling, but mature parents can control the feeling.

This attitude starts from the beginning and can get reinforced by many others, from family to strangers. I recall a time when we met at a restaurant with distant relatives from Sara's side of the family. These relatives were well-known for keeping a tight clamp on their boys (which actually led to many bad behaviors when the parents weren't around; again, see the next chapter for the reasons why!). But the parents' perspective was that they had raised model boys who would go on a visit, march in, sit on the couch, and keep their mouths shut—exactly what the parents wanted.

During this meal, one of my preschool children was very restless. They wanted out of their chair. They really wanted to roam around the table. They had eaten all they were going to eat, and the adult conversation was boring them.

Throughout this episode, the patriarch from Sara's family kept repeating, "You know, discipline begins at home!" I kept dragging my kid out of sight to scold them, threaten them, reward them, whatever it took for them to start behaving. Nothing worked.

I was still an inexperienced father. A couple of years later, I was able to stand up to my own father when he made similar comments during a zoo outing, but at this point, I just wanted to impress Sara's relatives. My child's behavior was reflecting on me, and I was embarrassed for myself. If the child had done the same things without these critical folks around, I probably would have reacted differently.

This is a case of caring too much about what others think. In this line of thinking, the child reflects on you, and your reflection is in this mirror called your child.

I've got to say, it's hard to overcome this thinking. It's hard to relax and let the child be themselves. Yes, you have rules that need to be followed, and the child shouldn't be a distraction, such as was happening during that meal.

But at the same time, you need to examine your own attitude and your own angst and try to find some comfort and confidence that in the long run, your parenting will be sufficient.

And that leads us to the next topic . . .

Peace in the Outcome

Raising a child from a helpless infant to a fully functioning adult is a beautiful mystery. It's an awesome responsibility. It goes slowly, and it goes by too rapidly.

Please believe that you have the ultimate parenting partner helping you: the Holy Spirit.

Another beautiful mystery is how the Holy Spirit fills in the gaps that we leave behind. It happens with prayer (Romans 8:26): **"We do not know what we ought to pray for, but the Spirit himself intercedes for us through wordless groans."** The Spirit helps by multiplying our meager efforts, such as Jesus did when multiplying a scant amount of food to feed more than five thousand people.

We have to trust that the Spirit is also raising our children, and this will give us peace.

One of the stories I share in my parenting classes regards a father, "Leonard," who was concerned because his adult children didn't turn out the way he had hoped; in particular, they weren't exactly faithful Christians. Leonard regretted this aspect of his parenting, worried about them, and felt guilty for his role. But his wife assured him that he had done everything he was supposed to do, and now it was in the Holy Spirit's hands. Indeed, in subsequent prayer, the Spirit revealed to Leonard that he had done his job of providing a Christian home and not to fret about it.

My rule for not having regrets in my parenting was to experience and enjoy every age of every child to the fullest. God made it so that children grow up at a certain pace. We can't stop that process. Instead, we should deeply experience the process alongside each child.

Despite being busy with my job and church volunteering, I was present and active with all my kids. My life was basically work, church, and family, and that was it. So I was involved in their sports and their scouting and their homework and their daily lives. I don't have regrets about not being present or involved or active at any point in their lives, so it's easier for me to have some peace in the outcome of my parenting and my relationships with my children.

To end this chapter on a unison parenting note, be dedicated as parents to enjoying and experiencing every age of your child. Be confident that the Holy Spirit will fill in the gaps in your parenting. Build each other up, even as you monitor and critique your parenting, so that you have a mutual, unison view of your child as satisfied parents.

I've alluded several times to the following chapter on **Supportive Parenting**. It's one of the most important in the book, as it refers to parenting styles. Your instinct as a parent is to fall into a particular parenting style—either the same or opposite of your parents—but it may not be a beneficial one. I'll examine the four types of parents and encourage you toward the ideal model.

Summary of Adaptive Parenting

Key Points

- Your child changes quickly. Plan to reintroduce yourself to this new person every six months or so and adapt your parenting to match. Tension with a child often comes from slow parental adaptation.
- Teaching your child to make decisions is one of the most important roles of a parent.
- Adapt your parenting to gradually give them more control over their decisions while limiting the consequence of bad decisions.
- The **Incremental Decision-Making** model proposes three phases for growing your child's decision-making capability as they age.
- Resist the urge to control your child or to see them as your reflection.

Unison Parenting Foundation

- Observe your child's behavior and communicate what you see to each other, so you can adjust your view of the child together as they rapidly grow and change.
- Agree on how you will apply the **Incremental Decision-Making** model. Stay in alignment as your child goes through phases. Agree on key principles of the model, such as letting your child fail and experience consequences in safe ways.

Supportive Parenting

Meditation: Ephesians 6:4

"Fathers, do not exasperate your children to anger; instead, bring them up in the training and instruction of the Lord."

If they are left solely to me, so many things in life aren't going to go well. Things go much better if I do them with God's help.

For example, in my book *Live Like You're Loved,* I share a story of how I learned to love a difficult person by praying, "Lord, if it's up to me, this won't end well. So please love this person through me. Let your love flow through me to them." The first time I encountered the person while praying in this way, things went a little better. There wasn't a dramatic shift in future meetings, but gradually, I noticed I was loving this person more naturally. It wasn't the grit-my-teeth experience that I first had. Later, Sara noted something I had missed; this person was starting to respond to my loving actions. It took some time, and I wouldn't say we ever achieved a close relationship, but there was certainly more love, considerate care, and tenderness in the room.

Similarly, the Ephesians verse above reminds us that if we parent according to our own rules and instincts, we are likely to cause resentment and division. We need to bring up our children with the discipline and instruction that comes from the Lord.

Let me be clear that I'm not talking solely about rules and commandments, but also the loving method by which the Lord teaches us. God is the perfect parent, balancing love and rules, righteousness and grace, free will and consequences. The laws of the Lord emerge out of God's love for us.

Similarly, our parental lawgiving must come from a place of love. Our discipline must be coupled with tenderness. Our instruction must not only be represented by what we say but by how we say it.

In doing so, we are more likely to avoid creating strife and dissension in our children. They will listen to us and love us back. Well . . . most of the time!

The Four Types of Parents

It's ironic that this chapter will rely on a decades-old model, yet what I have to say will likely be new, controversial, and hard to hear. In this chapter, I'm going to challenge your comfort level as you remember how you were raised, consider your own parenting style, and probably find out you've done a lot of things wrong so far.

> This chapter will rely on a decades-old model, yet what
> I have to say will likely be new, controversial, and hard
> to hear.

I've titled this chapter "Supportive Parenting" because the preferred model is considered the most supportive of the child's emotional development. I want to start with a well-respected academic view of parenting, then supplement it with real life examples of parenting gone right and wrong.

This model defines four parenting styles and describes what kind of children are produced by each style. As best as I can track down, the originator was University of California at Berkeley development psychologist Diana Baumrind in her 1967 analysis of how to predict preschooler behavior based on parenting styles. She defined three parenting styles: authoritarian, authoritative, and permissive.[14]

A fourth style, neglectful, was added in the 1980s by Stanford researchers Eleanor Maccoby and John Martin.[15]

I first learned of this model from Gary Smalley's book, *The Key to Your Child's Heart*.[16] Following Smalley's lead, I rearranged the term *authoritarian* to be *dominant*, and *authoritative* to be *loving and firm*.

The model is best described with this simple chart:

		Controlling Children by Limits or Rules	
		Low	High
Love and Support for Their Children	Low	**Neglectful**	**Dominant**
	High	**Permissive**	**Loving & Firm**

This is a quadrant chart, with each parenting style occupying its own quadrant based on two characteristics:

- Controlling Children by Limits or Rules at Home
- Love and Support for Their Children

The preferred parenting style, loving and firm, combines love and limits— love and support mixed with clear limits and rules. All other parenting styles have their flaws.

Let's walk through each style to understand it better and to learn of real-life case studies I have witnessed as a youth sponsor volunteer and as a teacher in fifteen years of parenting classes. As we do so, please be introspective as well about the style each of your parents exhibited, and what style you trend toward today. Kevin Shafer, PhD and associate sociology professor at Brigham Young University, confirms what many studies indicate: parents tend to follow the style with which they were parented, especially the dominant parent model.[17] Even so, it is not inevitable that we will follow the same style, as noted by Jay Belsky, a professor of child development at the University of California at Davis.[18] In fact, we may rebel against the style with which we were raised.

I hope you'll be honest with yourself; from what I described earlier in this book, you'll realize that I needed some work myself to move toward the optimal style.

The Dominant Parent

I want to start in the upper right quadrant because I feel like dominant parenting is the most ominous style since its short-term results look attractive and successful, but the long-term results can be devastating.

> Dominant parenting is the most ominous style since its short-term results look attractive and successful, but the long-term results can be devastating.

In each section, I'll provide a chart that shows key aspects of the parenting style, including what phrases tend to come out of the parent's mouth and what the children become as they grow older.

As you can see, the dominant parent indeed dominates the child's life. The child is treated as inferior, while the parent is superior. The child's opinion is belittled; this sometimes sounds like, "Who told you to think that?"—as if the child cannot think for themselves.

Characteristics of the children of dominant parents are:

- Being aggressive, but also socially inept and shy.
- Having poor self-esteem, rebelling against authority figures.

	Controlling Children by Limits or Rules		
Love and Support for Their Children		Low	High
	Low	**Neglectful**	**⎡Dominant⎤**
	High	**Permissive**	**Loving & Firm**
Description	**What They Say**	**What Their Children Become**	
• Very high standards and expectations • Few reasons given for rigid rules • May belittle child's opinion • Not much warm, caring support	• "Rules are rules. You're late – to bed with no dinner." • "I won't stand for your back talk. Apologize." (or slaps child's face) • "You don't need reasons. Just do what I say."	• Lowest in self-esteem / self-respect • Rebellious against parents or tending to clam up • Dismissive of parent's values; may group with other rebels • Potentially disruptive in class; may be demanding of their rights	

- Having difficulty managing emotions, resentful.
- Rarely learning to think on their own, having a hard time making decisions.
- Tending to become dominant parents themselves.[19]

What's interesting is that, on the surface, this style seems to work. Remember how I told you about my wife's extended family members who employed this method? If the family visited another household, the three boys walked in, sat down on the sofa, and kept their mouths shut. In the eyes of the adults, they behaved ideally.

Except . . . they didn't behave that way when Papa wasn't around. They were known as rebellious terrors in the community.

See the final column in the dominant parent chart. The children become rebellious. This may happen in either subtle ways or overt ways. Eventually, the grown child fights self-esteem issues because they are always told, either subtly or overtly, that they are stupid, ill-disciplined, easily manipulated, and need constant supervision.

It is truly startling to learn the hard way that a child has grown up in a dominant household. They eventually reveal themselves as two-faced, putting up a false, acceptable front, while revolting in the background in potentially harmful ways. Let me give you a few examples.

By far, my best-attended parenting sessions at my church were the Q&A's with high school seniors. As moderator, I asked them questions to prompt discussion, supplemented by parental questions. The goal was for the seniors to tell parents how things really are in the schools. Over the years, parents learned behind-the-scenes information like the uptake in vaping months before it became well-known (none of the adults had even heard of Juul), and that private Christian schools contained a lot more bad behavior than parents imagined; the parents might have Christian values, but the children didn't necessarily share those when around their peers.

But one of the more surprising admissions came from a senior boy, "Ronald," whom I thought was one of the best kids in church. Ronald attended practically every event when not occupied with his club sport; he was a leader; he seemed to be a friend to all, cutting across groups and cliques easily. Ronald always had a smile on his face and was always willing to pitch in.

During the parent Q&A, Ronald stated that parents should reward their children for good behavior by giving them more leash. Ronald was frustrated that he had abided by all his parents' rules perfectly, but they never relaxed any rules. For example, despite never giving his parents reason to worry and always arriving home before curfew, Ronald could never convince his parents to extend the time he could stay out. From being a sophomore with a fresh driver's license to becoming a senior leader ready for college, Ronald had never seen his curfew change.

Most worrisome was that Ronald had determined to punish his parents for it. "I never tell them anything about my life," he said. "I started doing things they wouldn't approve of. Nothing truly bad; just not what they would find acceptable. But to their view, I'm doing everything they want."

Ronald continued, "It actually hurts not to share my real life and my real feelings with them. But they would not accept what I truly think and who I truly am. So I put on a façade for them. They stay happy, and I do what I want to do, but I still get home on time."

How truly sad this is! Does this sound like someone who will have a tight relationship with his parents as an adult?

Even as a youth volunteer who knew the kids well, it was hard for me to distinguish the dominant parents. I got a feel for it from how the parents behaved, but it was harder to read in the kids—until they cracked in some way.

I remember a mother who had a daughter and son in the youth program at the same time, separated by a few years. She was the type who would some-times want to get the real scoop on how her kids were behaving. She was suspicious about them and sometimes a bit over the top with her meddling. I assured her that her children were behaving well in youth group.

And usually they were. But outside of youth group . . .

The first hint regarded the older daughter, "Jamie." She was a singer in the youth worship band. Jamie would sing her heart out, eyes closed with a beautiful smile, praising the Lord with song.

But another band member tipped me off that Jamie wasn't what she seemed to be. "Jamie's a partier. A **big** partier," he said.

It was hard for me to believe. But once Jamie left for college, I rarely saw a Facebook picture of her where she wasn't drinking or had alcohol in the picture, and she was not always looking sober. Jamie is married now; the same pictures continue. I'm not saying she shouldn't drink, but when you see picture after picture with alcohol prominently displayed, it makes you wonder if she's stuck in rebellion even now.

That might be a clue on its own to the mother's parenting, but then there is the son. "Joey" did not have the skill set to meet his mother's expectations and could never measure up to his sister's accomplishments. He struggled in the classroom. He would have to miss youth activities because he needed to study. Joey was quiet. He didn't seem to have many opinions when asked to partici-pate. If Joey did something kind, like write a thank-you note, it was clear that his mother's fingerprints were all over the gesture.

Once again, it was his peer group that tipped me off. Joey was smoking pot. He was drifting away from church. He was more disconnected from his studies. These boys weren't naïve; they knew a number of kids that smoked pot. But they were worried about Joey. They were also worried when Joey didn't have clear plans after high school.

In retrospect, I can surmise what was happening in the household, but I couldn't put it together at the time. That's the subtle, ominous effect of dominant parenting.

I've given you some relatively short-term outcomes; now let me share the story of "Annie," who in her sixties is still feeling the effect of her dominant mother.

Annie was an only child that grew up during the Vietnam War. Her father served in the military and was often gone in that period, leaving Annie's mother, "Norma," as her primary influence.

Perhaps Norma felt like she had to control things tightly without her husband around. More likely, she had learned the dominant parenting style from her father. For whatever reason, Norma became the quintessential dominant parent.

Annie could seemingly never do anything right. Her clothes were wrong. Her mother considered Annie overweight, even when she really wasn't. Every morsel that went into her mouth was observed.

If she held an opinion of her own, Norma belittled it. If Annie chose A, Norma told her B was correct. Then if Annie chose B, Norma would prefer A.

The kicker was when Annie earned her bachelor's degree in a nonscience field, but Norma destroyed the moment after the graduation ceremony by sighing and saying, "I always wanted you to be a doctor."

Annie's father didn't fulfill a key parental duty I'll be recommending later: he didn't hold Norma accountable. Worse, he pinned the family difficulties on Annie, telling her to "keep peace in the family" by apologizing to Norma even though Annie felt wronged.

Norma saw Annie through the lens of how Annie reflected on her (recall **Your Child Is Not a Mirror** in the **Adaptive Parenting** chapter). Annie was a talented musician; Norma would push her to perform for friends. Annie felt like a trained monkey, while Norma basked in the compliments.

Rebellion started swiftly when Annie left for college. Annie had always thought her family was normal, but now she realized that many of her fellow students didn't have to put up with what she did. That led to drinking, partying, and lots of sex. Driving from their home two hours away, Annie's parents walked into her dorm room unannounced one afternoon and caught her drinking with a young man.

Over time, Annie continued such behaviors but pushed them more to the background. She became a closet drinker, hiding it from her future husband. The habit would emerge from time to time, then return to its hiding place.

But on the surface, Annie seemed to be doing great, though she had a hard time making decisions. She had three kids, she enjoyed her job, she enjoyed her marriage, and she was active in her church.

Until the day Annie attempted suicide. Forty-plus years of pain couldn't be hidden any longer.

All sorts of mental issues started tumbling out and stacking up. Annie spent a lot of time in therapy, breaking down her relationships with her parents and how those influenced her today. At the core were self-esteem issues, as Annie considered herself worthless, even in the eyes of God—perhaps especially in the eyes of God. Her lack of self-esteem actually made Annie explosive, lashing out at anyone who had seemingly insulted or disparaged her. Relationships deteriorated; alcohol abuse escalated; suicide attempts returned.

It took Annie a long time to forgive Norma. Even in her failing years, Norma could hardly bring herself to tell Annie that she loved her because "Annie should know that already." When Norma died, it would seem natural to think Annie's nightmare was over. But it wasn't. Norma was still entrenched in her head, telling Annie that she was worthless and wrong, complaining about what lane she drove in, whispering that her family would abandon her because she was so useless.

Annie has achieved better mental health in her seventh decade, but will she ever completely rid herself of the effects of dominant parenting? That chapter is not written, but with a lot of therapy and a lot of love, Annie is finally starting to turn the page on the damage done to her as a child and teen.

Dominant parenting fails because it overrelies on limits and rules, served with a cold heart.

The Neglectful Parent

Let's slide over to the upper left quadrant to the neglectful parent, who also seemingly has a cold heart for their children but without the focus on rules. In fact, quite the opposite.

	Controlling Children by Limits or Rules		
Love and Support for Their Children		Low	High
	Low	**Neglectful**	**Dominant**
	High	**Permissive**	**Loving & Firm**
Description	**What They Say**	**What Their Children Become**	
• Stays away from children by doing own activities, frequent sitters • Lashes out at child when pushed or irritated • Occupied; often, all parents are working	• "Work it out yourself. Can't you see that I'm busy?" • "No! I'm expected somewhere tonight. Get your mother to help you." • "Good grief! Can't you kids be more careful?"	• Insecure and rebellious • Unable to control themselves • Lacking self-esteem because the parent seems to think they're worthless • Not motivated to do well in school	

The neglectful parenting style is more likely to be found in a single-parent home, in a home with two working parents, in a family that moves frequently, or with parents who are more absorbed in living their own lives independent of the children.

In many cases, the situation around the family may trigger this parenting style. But it's a parenting style that may also be utilized by someone not fully invested in serving as a parent.

Whether it happens by circumstance or by choice, it's a sad situation to witness neglectful parenting. Sympathy can be extended to the neglectful parent who has good intentions but little time because of various kinds of life situations. On the other hand, there are neglectful parents who unfortunately should not have been parents in the first place or should reorient their lives to be more present as parents: physically, mentally, and emotionally.

My view of this parent is that there is another thing they tend to say to the child. It is "_____." In other words, nothing. The parent may not be around the child. Or if they are, the parent is not fully present and may not even acknowledge the child.

> Neglectful parents tend to say to the child, "_____." In other words, nothing.

Examples of uninvolved parenting are:

- Ignoring their child when they are upset or crying.
- Expecting their children to care for themselves.
- Not respecting a child's interests.
- Failing to provide adequate supervision for a child.[20]

The result can be an insecure, uncontrollable, rebellious child. And their self-worth? Imagine not even being able to draw a response from your parent. The child figures out quickly where they rank in the parent's priorities.

Let's look at a few case studies of neglectful parenting.

My friend was a nanny for a two-lawyer couple. Their children were preschoolers. The parents worked tremendous hours, and when they were home, they were never far from the office—on the phone, on their computer, reading briefs, etc.

The nanny was almost a full-time nanny, spending at least eight hours per day with the children, fixing their meals, driving them to preschool, and sometimes working longer at the parents' request when they were hung up at work. Her feeling was that she rarely saw the parents engage with the children and that the children suffered from the lack of parental attention.

Because the relationship stopped after a couple of years, I have no long-term indication of the children's behavior. But I think about the stories the nanny told me and how the nanny held a higher place in the children's lives than the parents.

I got more insight—sometimes more insight than I wished—from a family that I knew that had gone through a nasty divorce. The parents constantly argued and fought over money, rules, and where the children would stay (not always following the court custody order). Each parent accused the other of poor parenting, and each seemed to do things to curry favor with the children at times.

In this case, the neglectful parent was the mother, "Ryleigh," who held custody of the three children. It became clear that Ryleigh was self-centered and played the victim. Everyone around her was at fault: the father, the stepmother, the children, and anyone who sided the least bit against her.

But often those critics had good reason. Ryleigh didn't perform a lot of the care that you would expect from a good mother. She was interested in dumping the kids so she could party, take trips, and have fun. There were times that the father considered calling the state child protective agency on her; in fact, he actually did call once, after an incident I'll share below.

It was hard to tell exactly what was going on in the household because everything was a smokescreen. But it was clear that the children were suffering. They each reacted in their own way. One daughter, "Sally," played the rebel. Another daughter played the substitute mom role. The youngest child, a boy, tried to stay out of the fray, but as he grew older, he rebelled in various ways too. He was found with drugs at one point.

Possibly the worst incident was the one that triggered the child protection call. Ryleigh came home from partying with a man and had raucous sex with him in the backyard pool. All the sleeping children were awakened and witnessed this event. Was it any wonder when a teenaged Sally repeated that performance with her own boyfriend?

Was it any wonder when the teenaged daughter repeated the mother's performance with her own boyfriend?

Our family had direct contact with a family in which both parents seemed, to me, to employ the neglectful parenting style. They had four children spanning a wide range of ages. It was chaotic to visit their house, as the parental oversight was light, and the parental enablement of unfortunate behaviors was high.

You never knew what would happen when you visited, which I did on several occasions. Once, their unsupervised youngest child had just blown up the microwave by putting metal in it and running it for, I don't know, an hour? No one was watching him. I can imagine that comment in the chart coming out of the father's mouth, "Can't you be more careful?" The same preschool boy would kick and curse at visitors.

The whole function of the household was chaotic. The place was a mess. There was no telling when dinner would be served. The father spent more time pontificating than parenting.

Once I was a counselor on a fifth-grade retreat during which the oldest, "Jeff," stayed in my team's cabin. On the first morning, I was organizing the boys to get dressed and be ready for breakfast at the camp cafeteria. I kept giving time checks, and I wasn't getting much action out of this kid. My rule was that a child could depart for breakfast once he had performed cabin chores and dressed for breakfast, so various boys would present themselves to me for approval.

I called out to Jeff at one point, asking if he was ready for breakfast. He said yes. When he appeared before me on the cabin porch, Jeff was wearing pants, no shirt, a sock on one foot, and a shoe minus a sock on the other foot. I asked whether he thought he was completely ready, and he said yes. I asked him, "Jeff, does your mother dress you every day? How on earth do you get to school?" In fifth grade!

From my perspective, things got worse once Jeff reached high school. The family house became party central, and the parents were at the root of it. They provided alcohol to visiting boys because "they're going to drink anyway, so it's better for them to do it here." (I'll have more to say on such a terrible policy in the **Teen** section.) The parties were out of control; the little terror I mentioned earlier was in upper elementary by then, drinking with the high schoolers.

I haven't kept up with the family to know how the kids turned out, but I do know that Jeff became a lawyer. They do grow up eventually! I wonder if Jeff was looking for some structure from the law after having so little structure around him growing up.

I realize these are worst case scenarios. So let me give a few examples that aren't quite as dire but still emotionally harmful.

My daughter had a friend, "Lily," a teenaged daughter of a neglectful single mother. When Rebecca started driving, it seemed like she was always late after a school event, hanging out with Lily. When I asked about it, Rebecca told me that Lily never knew when or if her mom was going to pick her up. Lily would wait sometimes up to an hour after a school event, the only person remaining, before her mother would eventually arrive. Helpful Rebecca would notify us of yet another stranding, then stay with Lily or eventually drive her home herself. (It was some distance to Lily's home, so on those evenings, Rebecca would arrive home quite late.)

Sometimes the mother was working, but more often, she was watching a show at home, talking to someone, or out somewhere. But Lily was stuck. She would call her mother, who would promise to come, then wouldn't. Or if Lily's mother would come, it was consistently later than promised.

I finally had a talk with Lily's mother to explain the impact of this behavior on both of our daughters. Things got better after that, but Lily still got stranded at times.

Besides the obvious danger, what is the emotional cost of being stranded by a neglectful parent? Or otherwise ignored? According to Dr. Jonice Webb, the child of a neglectful parent experiences these three challenges:

1. Lacking full trust in and love for their parents.
2. Feeling like their parents don't know them, although their parents should know them best.

3. Not wanting to be around their parents, to the point that the child convinces themselves that they don't need their parents' love and approval.[21]

When this happens, the child can overcompensate in other ways, as happened with my high school friend "Josh." His mother was neglectful and often absent, doing her own thing; his father worked distantly so that he would arrive home late. Josh's sisters would visit friends, so Josh was often left at home, eating dinner alone. I remember an Easter weekend when Josh was left in an empty house.

I saw that Josh would compensate for his lack of care by doing a couple of things. First, he would puff himself up to be more than he was. Josh tried so hard to make himself sound relevant and important in everything he did. Second, he would dominate conversations with a fully open faucet of sentences. It was hard to get a word in when Josh was speaking; he ignored cues to give others a chance to speak. In fact, it only made him talk faster and louder to keep control of the conversation.

Fatal flaws? Of course not. Did it cost him some friendships or some closeness with others? Yes. Ironically, what he needed were close relationships.

There's another way that neglected children needing close relationships can actually drive others way: by being clingy, needy, even "crazy" in relationships.

This is how author Krista Cantell said others described her in her relationships. It took some time for Cantell to realize that her "crazy neediness" stemmed from her childhood:

> *According to the principles of attachment theory, how we behave in our relationships—our attachment style—clearly reflects how we were cared for as children. Attachment styles are often formed from childhood, when you may have had a negligent caregiver. It completely resonated with me when I found this out because my parents essentially abandoned me.*[22]

Cantell goes on to say that as a child, she began to believe that she was the cause of her neglected state, not her parents. As a result, she suffered from low self-esteem.

According to Healthline.com, there is little upside to the neglectful parenting approach, though the writers acknowledge that children may become more resilient and self-sufficient out of necessity. But overall, kids raised under neglectful parenting suffer some of the worst outcomes when compared to kids of other parenting styles.[23] Children of neglectful parents exhibit these traits:

- Having trouble controlling their emotions
- Being likely to be depressed
- Having academic challenges
- Having difficulty with social relationships
- Being antisocial
- Being anxious[24]

The Permissive Parent

Shifting to the lower half of the table, we come to the permissive parenting style.

Love and Support for Their Children	Controlling Children by Limits or Rules		
		Low	High
	Low	**Neglectful**	**Dominant**
	High	**Permissive**	**Loving & Firm**
Description	**What They Say**		**What Their Children Become**
• Tends to be warm and supporting • Weak in establishing and enforcing rules and limits; child's experience is like leaning against a wall that seems firm but falls	• "OK, you can stay up late this time. I know how much you like this show." • "You're tired, right? A paper route is a tough job. I'll take you around." • "Please don't get mad at me. You're making a scene." • "Please try to hurry. Mommy will be late again if we don't start soon."		• Insecure • Possessing little self-respect; cannot control self or master discipline • Manipulative of people and rules; child senses they are in the driver's seat and can "play" the parent

From the point of view of a dominant parent, the permissive parent and the loving and firm parent look similar. But there are some key differences between the styles:[25]

Permissive Parenting	Loving and Firm Parenting
Always say yes to their children's demands	Say yes to their children's demands when they are reasonable
Dislike control over their children. They do not monitor or guide their children's behavior.	Dislike control over their children, but they monitor and guide their children's behavior
Have very few rules and standards of behavior. When there are rules, they are not consistently enforced.	Have some rules and standards of behavior. They are consistently enforced.
Let children make major decisions generally reserved for adult guardians without guidance.	Let children participate in making major decisions with guidance.
Place very little responsibility on their children	Place a sensible amount of responsibility on their children

The most significant deficit for the permissive parent's child is a lack of self-control. This can show up in various ways as the years go by:

- Worse academic performance
- More impulsive and aggressive
- More prone to delinquency, substance abuse, and alcohol abuse
- Worse social skills
- More likely to become overweight[26]

One way you can identify the child of a permissive parent is that they are negotiators. They don't take *no* for an answer because they have learned that they can turn the *no* to a *yes*. As I mentioned earlier, this was my early flaw as a parent;

on occasion, I would lapse into permissive parenting. I eventually figured out that I was training my children to negotiate with me, and I reasoned this could eventually carry over into their interactions with authority figures.

There is an insightful comment in the quadrant chart about how permissively parented children are insecure and feel like they are leaning against a wall that falls over. I've discovered in my interactions with my children's friends, as a baseball coach, and as a youth sponsor that such children would eventually respond surprisingly well to consistent discipline. They test boundaries and are displeased when they encounter firm boundaries, but they are secretly glad that those boundaries exist. Boundaries represent a different kind of caring.

On the other hand, a permissive parent lacks boundaries. Jane Nelson reports, "One mother told me that her child wouldn't eat anything except potato chips. I asked her where he got them. She exclaimed, 'Well, I buy them because he won't eat anything else!' Many children are being raised to be tyrants who feel they are significant only if they can manipulate other people into fulfilling their demands."[27]

Let's go to the case studies. I want to share two stories about children who visited my house and two that I encountered as their baseball coach.

"Ali" was not a good visitor. He aimed to do whatever he pleased, ignoring the rules of our household. Ali seemed like an affable guy, but he was going to do things his way, either overtly or covertly.

The way we dealt with Ali, though, proved my point above about consistent discipline. Visit after visit, we consistently stuck to the rules of our household, correcting him repeatedly about such things as the mess he was making, the way he treated others' possessions, or the way he responded to us parents. Ali didn't "get it" on the first visit or the second or the third. But over time, he fell in line with what we wanted and behaved better. Frankly, he even seemed happier to be doing so.

A striking corrective situation occurred with "Bobby," who came from a strange, mixed parenting environment. The parents had set up an authoritarian structure, but in their implementation, they veered toward being either permissive or neglectful. An incident happened at our house where the little negotiator within Bobby came out.

Some flap occurred between him and our two sons. I was trying to understand what had happened, but Bobby's story kept changing. The way my sons looked at me indicated Bobby was lying. So I used one of our favorite parenting techniques when disputes arose.

I said, "We're going to solve this in the way our family solves things. You three go into a room, close the door, and don't come out until you have **one** story. Then we'll decide what to do about it."

This is a powerful approach. When we used it with our children, the consistent result was that they came back with a very reasonable story of the sequence of events, what triggered the argument, how each reacted in order, and how they arrived at their impasse. Typically both children wound up taking some responsibility, though one usually admitted to being the main one at fault.

Well-schooled in this technique, our two boys broke Bobby down pretty quickly. In a few minutes, Bobby came back and explained what he had really done and how this was his fault. That day, he also learned the value of telling the truth and the possibility of mercy when you do.

Again, this is a case where having a structure and discipline caused the child to fall into line. By the way, we had no more problems with Bobby's behavior on subsequent visits.

As a Little League baseball coach in the recreational division, my job wasn't just to teach baseball but life lessons as well. "Hogan" needed some life lessons.

Hogan's behavior was erratic. He would pout if things didn't go his way or if he didn't have success. Or perhaps there would be an outburst. Or maybe his stomach would suddenly hurt. Anything might set him off. You tend to tiptoe around people like that.

Inevitably, his permissive mother got involved. She would sit him on the side or in the stands, cuddling and coddling. Sometimes Hogan would return to action, but other times they would pack up and head home.

Occasionally he wouldn't show up for a practice or game. His mother would explain it away somehow. Typically this would happen after an outburst at the prior team event.

After a while, I had seen enough. I told the parents that Hogan had an obligation to the rest of the team to be a team player and to behave like everyone else. He needed to decide whether he could abide by that.

Hogan decided he couldn't, and off he went. However, a couple of seasons later, Hogan and his parents asked if he could rejoin the team. While he still had a few tendencies like before, Hogan knew the rules and abided by them. He had a more enjoyable time playing baseball the second time around.

Years later, I coached a pitcher, "Reed," who came from a permissive household. In my estimation, the role of pitcher requires the most self-control of any position in sports. Even if you do your job, the fielders may not do theirs. Yet the pitcher is the focal point of winning or losing. The pitcher must have the self-control to move past disappointment with himself or others and focus on the next pitch, or things will fall apart.

Reed had little self-control. He had talent. But when anything went wrong, his self-control would start to spiral. His body language would turn sour, and his pitches would turn wild. His father wasn't much help to me in correcting the behavior. I had a lot of talks with Reed to try to help him grow, but nothing ever stuck for long.

Isn't it interesting how if you're not taught self-control and self-discipline, you don't possess self-control or self-discipline?

Isn't it interesting how if you're not taught self-control and self-discipline, you don't possess self-control or self-discipline?

The Loving and Firm Parent

Now that we have evaluated the lesser alternatives, let's learn the best alternative, a mix of love and limits.

Adding to the benefits listed above, children raised in a loving and firm household tend to be more self-reliant, socially accepted, academically successful, and well-behaved. They are less likely to report depression and anxiety, and less likely to engage in delinquency and drug use.[28] Another benefit you may have noted from my "one story" anecdote in the prior section: less sibling conflict.[29]

Love and Support for Their Children	Controlling Children by Limits or Rules		
		Low	High
	Low	**Neglectful**	**Dominant**
	High	**Permissive**	**Loving & Firm**
Description	**What They Say**		**What Their Children Become**
• Usually has clearly defined rules, limits and standards for living • Trains children to understand limits, warn them when they go beyond • Can be flexible with rules if exception needs to be made • Expresses physical affection • Spends time listening to child	• "Hey, I wish I could let you stay up later, but we agreed on this time." • "You're really stuck. I'll help you this time. Then let's figure out how you can do it yourself next time." • "You say all the others will be there. I'd like more info before I say yes." • "Did you practice piano? I hate to do this, but we agreed – no dinner before you're finished. We'll keep it warm for you."		• Highest in self-respect, respect of authority, interest in parents' faith, least willing to join a rebellious group • More content due to self-control • More secure; realize limits and why they exist • Willing to communicate well with parents, even through teenage years.

Loving and firm parents exhibit warmth and responsiveness with a dose of discipline, inspiring cooperation by fostering positive feelings and teaching kids the reasons for the rules. This differs from the drill sergeant approach of the dominant parent.[30]

Balancing love and limits is a tricky task and varies by situation. When do you focus on being loving, and when do you focus on being firm?

Two experts point us toward the loving option when in a quandary. Dr. Gary Smalley said to err on the side of love rather than limits.[31] Dr. Becky Kennedy blogs that when you must choose between connecting with your child or fixing their behavior, connect rather than fix. "We want our kids to associate us with being with them in their tough times. This association both strengthens our relationship with our child and helps a child build resilience."[32]

The case studies for the children of loving and firm parents are not as dramatic as the others, but they are much more rewarding. They are feel-good stories.

Seeing all sorts of kids in youth group, Little League baseball, visiting our household, and beyond, one characteristic of the children of loving and firm parents is that they are secure. They have a secure identity. They have a secure relationship with their parents.

They are not all extroverts. They are not all high achievers. But there is something really settled with them in how they carry themselves, how they interact with others, and how they interact with their families.

I'm remembering so many kids and families right now. Let me give a few images and memories.

"Molly" and her brother "Braylin" show up for our summer youth camp. I've never met them before. Molly is on my team, and Braylin is assigned to my cabin. As the week goes on, I see that settled nature in both of them, adapting to the stress of camp, having a calm approach to ups and downs, and being fully engaged in every activity.

When we return, they greet their parents warmly. As the family walks off together, you can tell Molly and Braylin have had a good time, but now they're truly home.

"Kevin" is a catcher on my Little League team. Big, stocky kid, home run hitter, coachable, great potential as a player. Unfailingly polite, Kevin comes up to thank me after every practice and game; his parents watch him with satisfaction from a distance and with only the occasional reminder to thank me. The family goes through tough economic times but with smiles on their faces and faith in their hearts.

Years go by without seeing them, and I find out Kevin isn't playing baseball anymore. His parents supported his desire to compete in bicycle off-road races; through diligence, Kevin has reshaped his body and has become a champion at his level.

The "Litrell" family's four children grow up and, one by one, take their place in the youth program. Every one of them is polite, pleasant, eager to contribute, and a friend to others. They're the ones that the church calls on to do anything from lighting candles in worship to appearing on a video to speak about the youth program or a service project.

But what is really impressive to me is how the children treat each other. The big sister, three years ahead of the next, isn't condescending. At summer camp, she checks regularly with her younger siblings without hovering. They have comfortable conversations. From the children's interactions, you can tell there's a lot of love and respect in the family.

When I see their parents with them, I sense this balance of love and limits. I witnessed it when they were growing up, before I actually knew them, watching the family sitting in the pews, the parents exuding this combination of warmth and discipline that produces these great kids.

The "Eriksson" family's four children all have distinct personalities, yet you can tell they were similarly raised. They possess servant hearts, high moral standards, passion, and self-discipline. They are active in school, church, and other activities, and their family has to accommodate four children going in multiple directions, but somehow you sense family still comes first.

This philosophy doesn't stop when they become adults. Although none of the four live in the same city, they regularly engage with their parents. They visit, or the parents visit them. The family is always communicating with each other. There are Mom of the Year and Dad of the Year awards just waiting to be handed to these parents, but perhaps great relationships with their adult children are the best reward.

I'll conclude the case studies by pointing to my own adult children. My parental peers are amazed when they hear that our family took a vacation together in Orlando this year, significant others included. We parents paid for the group's accommodation and a few other things, but everyone else had to pay their own way with flights, amusement park tickets, meals out, and more, so it wasn't a free ride by any means. Although it's not the first time we've traveled together, Sara and I feel great about our children's desire to vacation with us, but it doesn't seem abnormal. Meanwhile, many of our parental peers are saying their kids would never travel like that with them. I suppose we can take heart in the last statement on the quadrant chart, "Willing to communicate well with parents, even through teenage years." And apparently beyond.

What Does Love Look Like?

I realize that there hasn't been much direct discussion of love in this book. If you're wondering how to be more loving toward your children, the complete answer goes beyond the scope of this book, as that is a book (or a book series) of its own!

In the **Teen** section, I'll relate a story about how we used love languages to improve relationships within our family. As described earlier, this information comes from a series of books authored by Gary Chapman, based on his definition of five love languages and how to discern which languages are most important to a person.[33]

- Words of affirmation
- Quality time
- Receiving gifts
- Acts of service
- Physical touch

We've successfully applied these simple but profound concepts in our marriage and our family. While Chapman has written an entire series of love language books that I haven't read, I can vouch for the worthiness of the concept, a straightforward way to approach a complex topic.

Even though people typically resonate with giving or receiving in one or two languages, I suggest you utilize all five with your children. Yes, even the ones that don't work as well. Specialize in the ones to which they respond, but don't leave out the others.

For example, I would never rule out physical touch—hugging your kids. I have one child for whom physical touch has wavered in their love language priority and how comfortable they are with it. Nonetheless, they get a hug too! I just reduced the number of hugs when the trend was against physical touch,

but I didn't eliminate them, either. I want them to know that I will always hug them. Even to this day, everyone in our family hugs everyone else.

I suggest you also return to the Choices Chart and look at it in the light of the loving and firm parenting style. The Choices Chart never was a way to simply control children, but instead, it is designed to give them structure and discipline while also affirming their growing abilities and their fulfillment of family principles. You can imagine that as you become adept and natural at loving your child and bonding with them, it becomes easier to ask something back from them in terms of compliance and obedience, and they become more willing to comply and obey.

Is this not God's plan for the Lord's children as well? Love them but also ask them to obey. Our response is to obey and love God in return.

No Magic, No Guarantees

While the loving and firm parent style is the best, I must say that "your mileage may vary." Following this model does not mean your children turn out perfectly because of your perfect parenting. There are a lot of reasons for this.

Foremost is that humans can be inconsistent and mistake-prone. Even the loving and firm parent is going to slip up—and sometimes in large measure. Just as it takes a child a long time to build up trust with a parent, but just a moment to lose that trust, the same is true of a parent building and losing trust with a child.

Another factor is the individuality of each child. Some of that comes from personality, but some can be attributed to life circumstance. A child can be shaped by their overall environment, which includes experiences outside of the home.

A parental pitfall is mistaking the balance between love and limits, leaning on the wrong half of the equation when the other half is needed. Yes, in fifty–fifty situations, parents should lean toward love. But sometimes it's not a fifty–fifty situation, and a parent might incorrectly discern which side to lean on.

So there is no magic in this formula and no guarantee that your child will turn out exactly a certain way. That's why research uses terms like *tend to* or *more likely* or *best results*, not *always* and not *perfect results*.

I would apply the wisdom of the child seat commercial that says, "You're not going to get everything right. But get the big stuff right."

My adult children would tell you that I'm a great dad. But they also have a long list of complaints about my parenting decisions. I call it "the scroll," which they metaphorically unwind, letting the end tumble onto the ground, running off in the distance.

That's why Sara and I told our kids, "We'll pay for the counseling when you're an adult." And we actually have, at times.

Holding Each Other Accountable

Now I want to dig into a key topic of this book: holding your parenting partners accountable and vice versa.

I've presented the model for a loving and firm parenting style. I propose that you and your parenting partner(s) take the following steps:

- Study together the loving and firm style.
- Discuss how to implement the loving and firm style.
- Commit to following the loving and firm style.
- Agree to hold each other accountable when the loving and firm style is not followed, then do it.

> Holding each other accountable means that you should privately call each other out when one of you does not follow the loving and firm style, and gently bring that person back into alignment.

By holding each other accountable, I mean that you should **privately** call each other out when one of you does not follow the loving and firm style, and **gently** bring that person back into alignment, for the sake of the child.

Think about Annie's example and how her father put the family problems on her back rather than holding the dominant mother accountable. You can see why it's important to have an agreed model, then for a parent to call on the other parent to align with the agreed model.

It's tempting for parents to give up too soon when aligning with a new parenting style because the children will not necessarily align immediately. As Jane Nelson writes:

> *Children are used to getting certain responses from adults. When we change our responses, they will probably exaggerate their behavior (get worse) in their effort to get us to respond like we are supposed to. This is the kick-the-soda-machine effect. When we put money in the soda machine and a soda doesn't come out, we kick and pound to try to get it to do what it is supposed to do.*[34]

In addition, for a lot of reasons, the loving and firm parenting style may not feel natural to someone:

- They may have never seen it modeled anywhere.
- They were not raised by someone with that style.
- Their personality may lean toward another style.

However, those reasons should not stop someone from diligently trying to become a loving and firm parent. I hope I have proven throughout this chapter that other styles can do serious damage to children; if you are still unconvinced, please research further on your own. I appeal to you and your parenting partners to do what is necessary to help the child grow in the best possible environment. After all, isn't that why you are reading this book?

Look, even the best-intentioned parents are going to have bad days. We're going to get angry at our kids. We're going to carelessly make a mistake because we were distracted. We're going to misread a situation or make errors in judgment.

That's the time for a caring parenting partner to privately come alongside and gently point out how the loving and firm parenting style wasn't followed.

The off-target parent may already regret what they did, but they may also not realize that they were out of alignment. Perhaps there is some repair that can be immediately made, such as apologizing to the child or changing a decision. Perhaps there is nothing else to be done this time, but next time, the parent will be on higher alert to do better.

Speaking of apologizing to your child: it is not only acceptable but desirable for you to apologize to your child. From my own experience as a child, I can tell you how troublesome it is to realize that your parent will never apologize for their mistakes. This tendency is hurtful and is poor modeling. When I became a parent, I was determined to apologize to my child when I was wrong, and I have done it many times. I recommend it highly as a way to maintain the relationship, to soothe hurt feelings, and to model that no one is above making an apology.

> It takes emotional maturity and a strong will to both apologize to a child and to accept critique to become a better loving and firm parent.

It takes emotional maturity and a strong will to both apologize to a child and to accept critique to become a better loving and firm parent. I urge you and plead with you to demonstrate such maturity and will, for the sake of the child.

Reviewing Your Parents

Here's another tough topic: realizing your parents weren't perfect, forgiving them, and pressing forward to do the right thing in your own parenting.

Unless both of your parents were loving and firm, you must have seen the negative side of your parents in this chapter's parenting style descriptions. On the one hand, you might find yourself defending your parents from such critique. On the other hand, you may have had some realization of what they did wrong. Or perhaps, you already sensed that they damaged you, and now you're feeling negative emotion about your upbringing.

I would suggest that you wrangle with the ways in which your parents damaged you. You may need counseling. (Will they pay for it? I'm only half joking.) You may need to forgive your parents. You may need to dig into how your personality and habits have been shaped by your parents. You may even need to review the scroll of your parents' mistakes with one or multiple of them. (One of my adult children did that with me—a difficult experience, but ultimately freeing and helpful for both of us.)

This isn't the book to fully explore this topic, but I urge you to address your upbringing as needed—for yourself, for your parenting partner, and for the sake of your child.

Reviewing Yourself

I'll repeat what I said to start the prior section: it's tough to realize that **you** haven't been perfect, to forgive **yourself**, and to press forward to adjust **your** own parenting.

Many parents that read this book **should** realize they haven't aligned perfectly with the loving and firm model. Hopefully you've instinctively parented well. But this chapter forces a hard look in the mirror and a truthful approach.

Don't try to justify your mistakes. If you do, you will repeat them. Instead, use this chapter to correct those mistakes going forward.

This takes emotional and mental maturity. Sara and I joke about a repetitive *Happy Days* theme where Fonzie can't say the words "I was wrong." He gets stuck on "I was wrrrr . . ." When one of us admits a mistake, we frequently start with, "I was wrrrr . . ."

You may have to say, "I was wrong." I can't stress enough that I don't want you to beat yourself up, but I do want you to take steps for the sake of your child. Undeniably, some long-term damage may have already been done, but you can and will do better using the advice in this chapter. Just start putting aside some savings for that counseling!

If you're going to successfully provide a loving and firm parenting environment, you need to coordinate all of your parenting partners. In the next chapter, I want to acknowledge and examine different parenting situations, offering some tips on how to handle each from a unison parenting perspective.

For those of you in a traditional nuclear family situation, please don't skip the next chapter. I present some nuggets that will also apply to you. In addition, you most certainly will encounter families in other situations. Maybe you will learn something that will help them or will help you appreciate what they're facing.

Summary of Supportive Parenting

Key Points

- There are four parenting styles: dominant, neglectful, permissive, and loving and firm. The loving and firm model offers the best chance of children who have the most positive attributes/outcomes.
- The dominant, neglectful, and permissive styles actually can impose long-term damage on the child, extending into adulthood.
- Although it's not inevitable, many parents fall back on the styles modeled by their own parents.
- The loving and firm parent balances love and limits. When conflicted on which style to use, it's recommended to lean toward love and support.

Unison Parenting Foundation

- All parenting partners must become educated on the four styles to understand the impact of each on the child.
- Parenting partners must agree to align with the loving and firm style, for the sake of the child.
- Hold each other accountable, privately and gently, when deviations to the loving and firm parenting style occur.

Collective Parenting

Meditation: 2 Timothy 1:5

"I am reminded of your sincere faith, which first lived in your grandmother Lois and in your mother Eunice and, I am persuaded, now lives in you also."

If anyone in the New Testament had a complicated family life, it was Timothy, perhaps the apostle Paul's most trusted associate.

Timothy was born into a religiously divided and ethnically diverse household in Lystra, in southern Asia Minor. His father was Greek, while his mother was Jewish.

In his society, Timothy was considered gentile and was never circumcised, despite his mother's Jewish background. Yet his mother, Eunice, and his grandmother Lois had the most influence on his spirituality.

Raised Jewish, both women converted to Christianity, most likely during Paul's first visit to Lystra. As Paul acknowledged, the strong, sincere faith of these women prepared Timothy for his role as a leader in the fledgling Christian church.

Complicated families like Timothy's have become more and more common in modern society. Families now come in all varieties: those split by divorce or headed by a single parent (perhaps an always-single parent) or with same-sex parents or extending over generations and family tree branches to grandparents, aunts, and uncles. In fact, grandparents actually serve as the direct parents for many children.

This chapter addresses the many variations of today's family—and we'll hear from some of those families. I pray that, like Timothy's family, all these varieties of families are blessed and able to raise children who are responsible adults, trained in the Christian faith, and strong servants of Jesus.

The Rise of Nontraditional Families

Common sense and observation tell us that the nuclear family concept does not represent the majority of families in the twenty-first century. The data backs up that observation.

More than half of American children belong to families that do not match the traditional view of a father and mother in their first marriage. According to Pew Research Center's 2015 analysis:

- 46 percent of children live in traditional family environments.
- 26 percent live in single-parent homes.
- 15 percent live in families with remarried parents.

And aside from that, 16 percent, or one in six, live in homes where there is a stepparent, stepsibling, or half sibling.[35]

Same-sex couples with children are still fairly rare in the United States. According to the US Census Bureau's 2019 study, there are roughly seventy million opposite-sex partner households and one million same-sex partner households.[36] Of those, approximately 14 percent, or 140,000, same-sex partner households have children.[37] This accounts for less than 1 percent of all American children; observationally, that number appears to be slowly growing. Same-sex couples are seven times more likely than opposite-sex couples to have adopted or foster children in the home.

Interestingly, 37 percent of LGBTQ couples have had a child in their home at some point, indicating that many are parents to children who do not reside with them.[38]

It's not that unusual for grandparents to be the primary caregivers for their grandchildren. It's estimated that 5.7 percent of children live in a household with a grandparent; 3.6 percent are in a multigeneration household, while 2.1 percent live in a split-generation household, where the grandparents are the "parents" for the grandchildren.[39] In other words, roughly one in fifty of the children you see pouring out of an elementary school at the end of the day has a grandparent waiting for them who is the primary parent in their life.

All this data points to what we already instinctively knew: families come in a lot of flavors and varieties.

I want to spend a chapter dealing with the unique problems and unison parenting pointers for this broad array of families. I call this *collective parenting* to honor that it takes a team to raise a child—even in a single-parent home—and that team may not look like the traditional nuclear family.

Even if yours **is** the traditional nuclear family, I believe there are some interesting pointers in here for you or for families that you know. This chapter will give you a deeper understanding of the issues they face daily.

I will look at four family models in more detail and suggest how unison parenting principles apply to them:

- Families where divorce, and possibly remarriage, has occurred.
- Families led by a single mom on her own. This is a little different than the bullet before, as in this case, the father is no longer available because of death, imprisonment, or some form of abandonment.
- Families where grandparents fulfill the daily parenting role for the child.
- Families where same-sex couples serve as parents.

Divorced/Step Situations

Vitriol. Heinous manipulation of the children. A sexual assault of her daughter by a stepfamily member. When "Stella" and "Sam" split, things weren't too bad at the beginning. Sure, there were arguments and fights, but nothing like this.

As time went on, the animosity grew. Unhappy with living at Stella's house and enamored with Sam's lax parenting, teenagers "Paris" and "Clint" moved out of their mom's house to live with their dad. That's when things got worse.

Meanwhile, "Cindy" tells a similar story of feeling helpless when her elementary-aged son, "Theo," went to live with his dad, "Lonnie." Theo was permitted there to do very grown-up things too early, such as playing *Grand Theft Auto* at age eight. At the same age, Theo was given a cell phone—that had porn on it.

Now Theo is an older teen whose view of his mother has been poisoned by Lonnie's manipulation. Cindy mourns the years of fracture and how she will never retrieve the missing teen years with her son.

"Jon" got married at age twenty. Decades later, he admits he wasn't ready for either marriage or fatherhood. His image of fatherhood was providing for his family. Jon worked two jobs, while his wife did all the child care.

Jon admits to emotional immaturity as a young father. He didn't understand how to discipline or otherwise handle a child.

When he and his wife divorced when their daughter reached age eleven, Jon was left alone but with periodic visitation rights. He and his new wife were weekend parents and behaved that way. Everything was set up for fun: parties, camping, other outings. It wasn't designed to win favor with his daughter as much as it stemmed from the fact that he simply didn't know what to do with her.

These are the horror stories you might expect from families ripped apart by divorce. Still, there are also success stories of families where the parents put their children's interests first and tamped down their negative feelings to work together, in unison, to provide the best environment for the kids.

In this section, I want to travel along the journeys of several families to understand their situations (good and bad) and to extrapolate unison parenting pointers from them.

We'll take a look at divorced situations with no remarriage (yet), a remarried situation where the focus is on the children of the original married parents, and a remarried situation where two families blended, Brady Bunch–style.

Divorced, No Remarriage

"Aiden" and "Brooke" went through a bitter divorce that was capped by a year-long custody battle. Six months past that, they share equal parenting time but basically don't share conversation. When they attend soccer practices and games of nine-year-old son "Danny," they ignore each other.

Aiden says he doesn't want to talk to Brooke about parenting practices. He calls it *parallel parenting*, in which he does things his way, and she does things her way. With Danny approaching an age of greater awareness, it seems like only a matter of time before this conflicting parenting style and attitude negatively affects him.

On the other hand, "Caplan" and "Crissy" have been divorced for about a year now. Their last child at home, "Ewen," is a high school senior who splits time between parents. Their parenting of Ewen is in sync.

"We had a parenting structure, and we kept it," says Caplan. "Friction that got in the way of the parenting structure when we were married is now gone, so our parenting is actually calmer and more in sync than in the last years of our marriage."

Caplan says once you're divorced, the only reason to talk to each other is your child, so you can focus on that issue alone. Caplan and Crissy have been able to communicate frequently on Ewen's situation, including his college plans, and have encountered few disputes.

"You have to guard against third-party issues," says Caplan, referring to other issues that impact parenting, such as you or your ex trying to manipulate the child. "You have to watch out to not project your issues onto the parenting situation."

Divorced parents should collaborate, not manipulate.

Caplan's theme is "Collaborate, not manipulate" when it comes to successful divorced parenting.

Stella (introduced earlier) has not been so lucky with Sam, as manipulation has been frequent. Stella says, "It works best when you can compartmentalize—keeping your relationship issues out of the parenting activities."

In such a scenario where parents are not cooperating well, Stella finds "you have to pick your battles regarding the kids." She fought hard for choosing the right ADD medication for Clint but gave in to Sam's desire to force the children to attend his church. (Stella does not attend church, and the children didn't want to start going.)

Throwing up her hands at the conflicts she and Sam continue to have, Stella says, "It's better to have no expectations of your ex."

But unison parenting says we should indeed have expectations of each other as parenting partners. Caplan and Crissy have it right; put the personal issues aside and just focus on being the best possible parents for the children. Collaborate—don't manipulate.

Divorced, Two Remarriages
"Stan" and "Glenda" divorced when "Greg" was in middle school and "Hudson" in elementary. It wasn't too long before Glenda married "Richie," which took Stan by surprise. A few years later, Stan married "Elaine."

From previous marriages, both Richie and Elaine have children that do not live with them. Richie's children either live with their mother or are adults, while Elaine's children are all adults.

Because of this, neither Richie nor Elaine have much to say about the parenting choices that Stan and Glenda make, simply adhering to the policies established for the children. This makes it easier, as they are parenting partners who stay out of key decision-making. However, Elaine does feel some frustration as she would like to be a mom to Stan's kids and establish authority, but her role is more of a friend.

Stan reports that he and Glenda generally get along, especially in terms of parenting. They too have retained the parenting framework from their marriage.

Parenting partners can play different roles and can shift roles.

One wonders as these families move forward if Elaine's frustration will rise and become a factor. This is not impossible to address. Parenting partners can play different roles and can shift roles. If a parenting partner wants to become more vocal, they could be included in discussions—probably not to the wide scope of the original parents but certainly on behaviors, policies, and relationships within their own households. Elaine may also benefit from coparenting ideas at the end of the next section, regarding what boundaries she can and can't cross.

It's possible for Elaine to get more involved while Richie stays less involved, although one could foresee a situation where Glenda might want to balance the parenting power between households.

Divorced, Remarried as a Blended Family

You may need a program to keep up with the participants in this complex situation!

- In the blended family, "Flo" is the wife, and "Dayton" is the husband.
- Flo's ex-husband, "Allen" is remarried.
- Dayton's ex-wife, "Melanie," has not remarried.
- Flo and Allen had one child, "James," who has been shared in a joint-custody situation. They divorced when James was seven.
- Dayton and Melanie have two children, "Ella" and "Jacques," both in elementary when they divorced. Both went to live with Melanie; Dayton hosted the children every other weekend. After Melanie moved out of state, they moved in with Flo and Dayton.

Whew! It's all relevant, so I wanted to clarify.

After divorcing, the situations with the exes were very different. Flo and ex-husband Allen got along well. Before she remarried, Flo's job caused her to travel unexpectedly. Allen and his wife were very flexible in adjusting schedules to keep James. There were never any serious challenges, and Flo and Allen kept and evolved the same parenting framework as when they were married.

Dayton and ex-wife Melanie had a vastly different relationship. Melanie suffered from "adult issues" and was irresponsible. She and Dayton clashed a lot.

Let's move to the time when the families became blended, with three children in the household. Dayton's children, Ella and Jacques, were eleven and nine, respectively. Flo's son, James, was nine.

Flo says that having Dayton's two children full-time revealed issues that weren't evident when they visited every other weekend. For example, she began to see Dayton's hands-off approach to his children's emotional needs. With ex-wife Melanie geographically distant and Dayton aloof, Flo felt like she had to step in to address matters such as Ella was experiencing with puberty.

However, Flo felt she never had permission to be a stepmom. Both Dayton and Melanie erected barriers to keep her out of their children's lives, which was difficult as Flo is a nurturer by heart.

A worst-case scenario developed: inconsistent rules. There were different parenting frameworks for the children in the blended family.

Because of these barriers, a worst-case scenario developed: inconsistent rules. James had one set of guidelines with Flo, and Ella and Jacques had another with their divorced parents. James had his own set of emotional issues that required loving discipline, so Flo tried to straddle behaving one way toward two children in the household and a different way toward the third. But she found that so difficult that often she applied the Ella and Jacques framework to James, to his detriment. Rhythms, rules, and how love and frustration were expressed did not match James's framework nor needs.

Fortunately, ex-husband Allen stayed in step with Flo on what was happening and tried to provide, from his end, the support James needed.

In the first year or so after Ella and Jacques came to the household, they were open to her efforts, but over time, ex-wife Melanie sufficiently undermined Flo's standing so that all Flo could be to them was a mother figure instead of a mother. (Of course, she wasn't their mother.)

Relationships deteriorated. Ella returned to live with her mother. Even though they attended church together, Flo and Dayton were drifting apart and toward toxic silence. Flo insisted on marriage and parental counseling with Dayton; it unveiled irreconcilable differences. Ultimately, Flo saw a growing need to do what was best for James and decided to divorce Dayton.

Flo has done a lot of self-examination since then, trying to understand what could have gone better. Here are some of her reflections.

- The ingredients of a good marriage are the same as they are for good parenting. It starts with selflessness and an understanding of what each wants out of the relationship. Preconceived notions need to be identified.

The ingredients of a good marriage are the same as they are for good parenting. It starts with selflessness and an understanding of what each wants out of the relationship.

- Personalities play a big factor. Flo realizes that a "driver" like herself needs to let go and simply be on the journey. She tried to compensate for what the other parents weren't bringing and had her preconceived notions of what Ella and Jacques needed; maybe they didn't need what she thought. Perhaps she simply should have been available for them when things went haywire.
- We have an idealized version of *The Brady Bunch* in our heads, where two families blend seamlessly, for the most part. Instead, some days there is bonding; some days there is chaos.

Removing marriage from the equation actually allowed all three kids to reset, and they were able to be friends with each other after the divorce.

I asked Flo to propose what blended families can do. She responded with:

- From the outset, undergo counseling with all four blended family parents involved.
- An outcome of counseling should be an agreed framework for all the children that is focused on the welfare of the children. Even if a parenting partner strays later, there is a framework with which to bring them into alignment.

From the outset, undergo counseling with all four blended family parents involved. The outcome should be an agreed framework for all children that is focused on their welfare.

- Good communication between parents on an ongoing basis is essential. Flo envisions a scenario of attending a parent-teacher meeting for Jacques that Dayton could not attend, and asking ex-wife Melanie, "How do you want me to handle the meeting to represent you? What questions do you have for the teacher?"
- As the child changes (e.g., puberty), have more parental discussions about how to adapt to the new reality.
- Parents should be more vulnerable with acceptance of the principle that kids should be the center of the parenting effort rather than the parents' needs.

My own reflection on Flo's suggestions is how much her recommendations aligned with the previous chapters in this book.

- Having an agreed parenting framework. (Proactive)
- Identifying new situations and communicating between parenting partners. (Reactive)

- Adapting to change as the child changes. (Adaptive)
- Bringing a parenting partner into alignment when they stray from the agreed plan. (Supportive)

I have one more unison parenting pointer for blended family parents: to understand where the fence is.

As an example, in my youth ministry years, I became involved with several families that needed friendly outside help. I had plenty of conversations with their children. I realized there was a line I could not cross regarding the child's decision-making and their family dynamics; the parent always had control, not me. My role was to ask questions, supply answers when asked, and offer support and a listening ear. For the blended parent that feels tempted to do more but can't, those are good guidelines to follow as well.

Single Moms

"Moriah" thought life was going well and always would. She had two young boys and a husband, "Ray," who was active in their church. They lived in a big house in a nice neighborhood. She was able to stay at home with the boys for the most part, working a few hours in a part-time job.

Then came Ray's fortieth birthday. First there was a big birthday blowout to celebrate. Then came the family blowup. Experiencing a midlife crisis, Ray abandoned the family, began doing drugs and engaging with prostitutes, and Moriah was suddenly a single parent of two boys in shock.

Not only was Moriah a single mom, but because of her husband's situation, he wasn't (nor was he interested in) serving as a father anymore. The divorce eventually happened, but well before that, she was truly a mom on her own.

While this is an extreme case, I want to devote a section to single moms whose children do not have a father in the picture. In my years of working with church youth, the vast majority of single parents I encountered were women. Their cases seem different to me than the traditional divorced parents I discussed earlier. Such women faced situations such as having a:

- Deceased husband.
- Imprisoned husband.
- Husband who had literally disappeared and could not be found.
- Husband who was toxic for the children to be around; there are many reasons this could happen.
- Husband who divorced, moved to another state, and had no interest in remaining in contact with his family.

As I mentioned a few paragraphs ago in the **Divorced** section, sometimes I was privileged to get involved in such families to help out the single mom. Wise and cautious, yet trusting, they allowed me to partially fulfill the male role as a father figure or as a big brother to their child. Based on those experiences, I have some suggestions to share for the abandoned single mom and children.

Be Open to a Male Role Model

To continue the point in my last paragraph, it might be essential to look outside the home for help in serving all the children's needs. Imagine a single mom who has all the parenting duties and all the income responsibility thrust upon her. How can she sanely fulfill all the roles? Adding a male role model can help.

I advocate for this plan in the **Preventative Parenting** chapter later, in regard to young teen girls, based on their innate need for a father figure (which, I guarantee you, they will find on their own, if you do not provide one!). But as I describe more deeply in the upcoming Same Sex parenting section, children need a balance of safe haven and secure exploration. It's possible for one person to provide both, but it's difficult. If you are wired to provide a safe haven, then you'll want some sort of partner or role model to encourage secure exploration in your child. Or vice versa.

> With monitoring, it's possible to provide a safe environment for a male role model to help with your child.

On the negative side, there is always concern about opening up the child to manipulation or abuse. With monitoring and a plan in place, it's possible to reduce the possibility. For example, one rule I had when taking a child out of the house was to have a clear agenda with a clear timeline, and the ability of the mother to check in with her child at any point, either on my phone or theirs if they had one. Using safe word techniques I discuss elsewhere, the mom could determine if everything was going all right.

I also shared information with the mother regarding what I had learned from being with the child. I did not always share everything, depending on confidentiality and trust with the child, but I did share what the mother needed to know and hinted (if needed) at areas of improvement or concern. (Danger, of course, is always revealed to a parent.)

The outside person could also be a family member. For example, Moriah benefited from an uncle who partially filled the father role for her children, despite living out of state.

Remember that the male is also at risk, as your child or someone else could raise a false accusation against him. Develop policies that benefit and protect both parties, and clearly express how those will make everyone safe.

Finally, let me say that a parent, especially a single mom, will naturally worry about putting their children under someone else's care, male or female. There are trade-offs; clear benefits are weighed against danger concerns. I would recommend finding ways to achieve the benefits while addressing danger concerns, rather than secluding your children from others. Your children need those interactions, and you could use the assistance from the village around you.

Start Therapy Early

This may seem an easy thing to say but a hard thing to do, especially when the family now faces an economic crisis after father abandonment or death. But I think it's very important, as the children will experience abandonment issues, and their feelings need to be expressed. Both family therapy and individual therapy, including for the mother, are important. Look for free or reduced-cost therapy in your area.

It's not unusual for children to react differently depending on age. In the case of "Latricia," her eldest was able to adapt better than her youngest; the same went for Moriah and her kids. In both cases, the eldest was more mature but also felt a ton of responsibility to uphold the family. Thus, they might seem fine on the surface but could use a safe place to work out their emotions.

One disturbing trend to monitor is a child justifying bad behavior because of what happened to them. For "Janine," her middle child, a boy, used the breakup and abandonment as justification for misbehaviors that eventually escalated to crime.

Another pattern to consider is how the child's negative traits may become amplified. Moriah's younger son had anger issues to begin with; these only increased after his dad abandoned him.

Don't Beat Yourself Up

Single moms can feel so guilty. They can take on some of the guilt of the abandonment. They feel overwhelmed and feel like they're not making the best decisions. They don't have the time and money to give their children the childrearing experience they had envisioned.

I hope it's welcome to hear "Don't worry." Give yourself some grace to not be the perfect parent. You're going to make mistakes. You're going to get tired and frustrated with your children. Just try to limit the mistakes and frustration as much as possible, then apologize when needed.

Try to avoid getting overwhelmed. Talk things over with a trusted friend or family member, using them as a sounding board for parental decisions, time conflicts, and kid drama.

Ultimately, this is a time for prayer and faith.

Ultimately, this is truly a time for prayer and faith, you and your family getting closer to the Lord, holding onto each other while also clinging to Him, listening to His voice, praying for strength and guidance, and waiting expectantly for Him to lift you up on wings like eagles. A faith community can be immeasurably helpful in supplementing what God provides or being His vehicle.

Grandparents as Parents

"Monty" is trying to break his granddaughter "Chloe's" bad habit of taking food to her bedroom, eating part of it, and leaving it out to rot. Three-year-old Chloe is starting to catch on to the concept, though. Whenever she sees Monty opening the refrigerator, she says, "Don't waste the food!"

Chloe lives with Monty because her mother/his daughter, "Carolyn," has been through a rough spell that continues. Carolyn is divorced; Chloe's father is addicted to drugs and doesn't pay child support; and Carolyn has battled bouts of depression, joblessness, and general life instability. Monty had to take over Chloe's care at the age of two.

Carolyn bounced around for a while before moving into Monty's house seven months ago. But she hasn't taken over any parenting duties; in fact, she tends to ignore Chloe and wants to move out again someday to truly be on her own, which she has never done because of marrying at a young age.

Meanwhile, "Craig" and "Louise" also have their daughter, "Madison," living with them while they serve as primary parents for Madison's twelve-year-old daughter, "Maria," who was born addicted to drugs. When Madison's drug addiction overwhelmed her seven years ago, Craig and Louise took over five-year-old Maria's care and moved out of state, away from Madison and toward their other children. Madison has since gotten clean and moved in with them. They remain the primary caregivers, with Madison only giving opinions in the background.

It gets more complicated. Craig and Louise have six other grandchildren who live nearby. For the older ones, it was always hard to understand why Maria received bigger gifts and special treatment from their grandparents. Even their own adult children were jealous of the attention Maria received as, in effect, a new, much younger sibling of theirs. Craig and Louise have had to carefully navigate those emotions while making sure Maria receives all the loving parenting she deserves.

These two families serve as examples for understanding the issues that come when grandparents must take over the care of their grandchildren. I want to discuss some of the problems they face, along with ideas for the complicated unison parenting scenarios that exist.

Challenges of Parenting as Grandparents

The American Association for Marriage and Family Therapy lists the following challenges for such grandparents:

- Legal: Custody/guardianship, school enrollment, medical care.
- Financial: Limited financial resources, especially if they have difficulty supporting themselves.
- Parenting: In addition to parenting a second time around, the children often have emotional, behavioral, and physical difficulties.
- Physical and Mental Health: Grandparents may have limited energy and physical health issues. Adding a grandchild in the home can lead to anxiety or depression.
- Social: Less time for themselves, partners, and friends. Social connection is already a key issue for the elderly.
- Family Relationships: May experience conflicts with and need boundaries for the child's parents. Other adult children and grandchildren sometimes dislike the amount of attention being given to one part of the family or may be concerned about the impact of raising grandchildren on the grandparent's physical and mental health.
- Accessing Services: Lack of awareness, lack of transportation, or personal health and mobility issues can get in the way.[40]

Several of these were primary concerns for the two example families. Let's delve further into aspects of parenting, physical/mental/social health, and family relationships.

Aligning Collective Parenting Partners

From a unison parenting perspective, the key question is how grandparents can partner with the parents from whom they have inherited the child. This seems like an area fraught with peril.

Generally speaking, both families have navigated this partnering without too much difficulty. In both cases, the mother has had little interest in resuming her direct parenting. But, of course, the mother's mind could change in the future.

In Monty's case, Carolyn has not wanted to engage with Chloe in much of any way. Monty describes Carolyn as irresponsible and neglectful, telling Chloe to "leave me alone" or "play in your room" if she interrupts whatever Carolyn is doing. Naturally, three-year-old Chloe gravitates to Monty, who pays attention to her.

There is little discussion of parenting framework. Monty sets the framework, the limits, and especially the routine, which has proven to be essential for Chloe's well-being and development.

In Craig and Louise's case, there is no question that they are the parental figures for twelve-year-old Maria. Now that Madison has moved back in, the relationship between her and Maria is more like sisters. Nevertheless, Maria clearly understands who her birth mother is.

Madison still has opinions on Maria's upbringing but is grateful for her parents' sacrifice and does not interfere. She defers to their judgment but does express her views in private. Because Maria struggles with anxiety, Craig and Louise include Madison in discussions of how to approach treatment.

Madison considers the current living arrangements temporary and plans to move out someday, but all parenting partners agree that Maria will not be going with her.

The only conflict is over what happens to Maria if both grandparents pass away. Their will states that an agreeable uncle and aunt will take over her care. Madison doesn't like this and has requested her parents to reconsider their decision, as she would like to parent Maria in that instance.

> It helps when there is a clear center of control, and all
> decisions are made with the sake of the child in mind.

It's clear that both families are fortunate. There could have been a lot of infighting with the birth parents, and that potential remains. It helps that there is a clear center of control at present, and all decisions are being made with the sake of the child in mind. In both cases, the grandparents are cautious to relinquish control unless they are convinced the birth mother has earned it.

One unison parenting point is that the child's welfare and stability come first, and parenting partners must align around that priority.

Another unison parenting point is that a clear pecking order, if you will, must be established. In these families, the grandparents serve as primary decision-makers, and any input from birth parents is advisory. However, in other families, another model might allocate more input and decision-making power to one or both birth parents, and the grandparents would execute those decisions, probably with latitude on how the big picture is implemented on a daily basis. Much like the decision-making patterns discussed in the upcoming **Collaborative Parenting** chapter, a grandparent might gradually cede more control and power to the birth parent as they prove their stability and wisdom.

> Defer to the grandparents. Show respect for how they've
> laid down their lives for the child, and offer support.

Craig and Louise offer this advice to birth parents: Defer to the grandparents. Show respect for how they've laid down their lives for the child, and offer support.

Physical, Mental, and Social Self-Care

Both families expressed the difficulty in maintaining their physical health while taking on a heavy parenting load and trying to keep up with their grandchild.

Things they could do in their first go-round as parents—such as playing on the floor or playing catch in the yard—are difficult or even impossible. Kids can keep you young, but they can also make you feel old as you experience aches and pains in trying to keep up.

Perhaps even more vital are the mental and social health aspects, especially reacting to loss of social connection. Grandparents can feel isolated and that they are the only ones experiencing this.

For Craig and Louise, a grandparent support group at their church provided a friendly network and eye-opening results. They found their own situation better when comparing to a single grandmother caring for four grandchildren!

Craig and Louise felt equipped to parent but quickly realized that they needed to compare notes with other grandparents.

Monty admits to some loneliness, as he has no such support group. He will retire soon, which will also diminish his social network.

Family Relationships

Earlier, I alluded to the jealousies that arose in Craig and Louise's extended family after they took in Maria. Let's get into more details.

First, imagine Christmas. The grandchildren in another family would receive primary, larger gifts from their parents and secondary, smaller gifts from Craig and Louise. But these other grandchildren saw Maria receive primary, larger gifts from their grandparents. They felt like they were being treated worse than Maria, when they felt all grandchildren should have equal status.

This led to frank conversations with the other grandkids about Maria's needs. Craig and Louise assured them that if the other grandchildren's needs would ever grow to the size of Maria's, they would make sure to respond.

Interestingly, there was some reverse jealousy as well. Louise has a pet name for Maria. One day, Louise used the same pet name with a younger cousin. Maria didn't respond well, saying she wanted special status.

More complexity happened with the prior generation. Louise and Craig's own children felt jealousy with Maria and anger with Madison for creating the situation.

It would have been easy for Craig and Louise to get out of unison with each other when faced with these competing priorities. However, they have remained steadfast in their prioritization of Maria, their love for their grandchildren, their renewed support for Madison, and their desire for support while giving up a portion of their lives to address the current needs of their children and grandchildren.

Final Thoughts from Grandparents

Is parenting harder or easier the second time around? From the aspect of how they directly deal with their grandchild-in-the-house, both sets of grandparents say it's easier.

Monty says he is more mature than he was as a first-time parent and is doing a better job as a result. Craig and Louise say they are more relaxed this time; they were stricter with their children. In retrospect, they can see that they were too controlling, which led to issues for their children as adults, particularly in their faith walks. For example, their children were not allowed to listen to secular music, but Maria is.

Craig and Louise also find themselves in better sync and unison. They talk things out in private, and if one of them gets a bad feeling about anything, they will call for a private session to hash things out.

In terms of what advice they would give to other grandparents:

- Craig pointed to having a network of support, such as a church group of similar grandparents. As stated earlier, it's important to realize others are in the same situation and to be able to compare notes.

Find a network of support to meet with other grandparents in the same situation and compare notes.

- Louise reminds grandparents to lead with love; if they are considering love vs. discipline, err on the side of love. Even through all the issues emerging from Maria's drug-addicted infancy, they have put love foremost.
- Monty cites the daunting task ahead for a grandparent, especially emotionally, when you have planned to coast through this phase of life but now have daily responsibilities to a child. But he reminds himself how different Chloe's life would be if he were not there to stand in the gap and give her an edge for the future.

If you're a grandparent raising your grandchild, please refer to the **Useful Links and QR Codes** section for further ideas on raising grandchildren.

Same-Sex-Led Families

I'm going to lead this section with a spoiler summary based on facts and research.

- In societies where there are negative perceptions of same-sex-led families, children experience poor outcomes scholastically and emotionally.
- In societies where same-sex relationships are not only legalized but accepted, children of same-sex-led families either match or outperform their peers in families led by heterosexual couples.

I'll share the research momentarily, but I want to first highlight that the biggest parenting challenge for same-sex parents could be dealing with how the children may be negatively viewed by others.

There is another significant issue for same-sex parents that I'll address later in this section, regarding how typical gender-based functions are provided to the children.

The Research and the Challenge

As I mentioned before, some research about same-sex parenting is bleak. Here is a sampling:

- Graduation rates are lower for children of same-sex parents, who are only 65 percent as likely to graduate high school compared to children of opposite-sex parents.
- Emotional problems are more than twice as prevalent for children of same-sex parents compared to children of opposite-sex parents.
- Attention-deficit hyperactivity disorder is more than twice as prevalent in children of same-sex parents.
- Women (average age: twenty-nine) who grew up with gay or bisexual fathers experienced more adult attachment issues—less comfortable with closeness and intimacy, less able to trust and depend on others,

and more anxiety in relationships—compared to those raised by heterosexual fathers.

- A large, groundbreaking 2012 study from the University of Texas at Austin found that young adult children (ages eighteen to thirty-nine) of parents who had same-sex relationships before the children had reached adulthood fared worse than young adult children from heterosexual families in seventy-seven of eighty outcome measures.

In addition, generally speaking, when studies included the opinions of the same-sex parents compared to the opinions of their adult children, the parents presented a rosier view than the adult children did as all reflected on the children's upbringing and subsequent adult results.[41]

These are tough statistics to face if you're in a same-sex parenting situation. However, there are some interesting counterstudies from locations with more acceptance of same-sex couples.

- A study in the Netherlands suggests no significant disadvantages for children with same-sex parents compared to different-sex parents.[42]
- A Belgian study by local university KU Leuven found that children from same-sex couples are 6.7 percent more likely to graduate than children from different-sex couples.[43]
- A study by BMJ Global Health, released in March 2023 and drawing from thirty-four studies over thirty-three years in countries that legally recognize same-sex relationships, concluded that children of same-sex parents fared as well as children from opposite-sex parent families on a variety of metrics, including physical health and education outcomes.[44]

For same-sex parents, a huge challenge is how to raise children and adolescents who may be looked down upon because of their family classification.

Thus, it seems that the environment around a same-sex-led family has an impact on the children's performance. For same-sex parents, a huge challenge is how to raise children and adolescents who may be looked down upon because of their family classification.

How to Prepare Your Family

Children of same-sex parents may encounter bullying and ridicule in school, particularly in the late elementary and middle school years, as they navigate new social hierarchies.[45] So this is an especially good age to prepare your child for what they might encounter.

Simply explaining relationship status and family makeup to school professionals, medical professionals, and friends or parents of children is difficult.

Dr. Bethany Cook, a clinical psychologist and a same-sex parent, gives three ideas for equipping your children.[46]

First, never lie to them. Cook says, "When a kid first notices that their family looks different than some of their friends' families, you might have to field some hard-hitting questions. If you're tempted to omit information, gloss over the details, or outright lie, don't."

"Meg" and "Sherry" are lesbian parents who married after Meg divorced her husband and brought her kids along with her. Meg says the key is, "Be open and above board." For their case, Meg and Sherry say that the adjustment for the kids was not as big because they were aware of Meg's bisexual history. A bigger adjustment has been the bitter divorce that Meg experienced and the ongoing battles between Meg and her ex-husband.

Cook advises keeping conversations about family structure basic and matter-of-fact. "Stick to simple, black and white language, as if you were teaching them how to fold a towel."

Second, give them a script for talking to other kids. A couple of Cook's examples of what to say when others ask about having same-sex parents:

- "I have two moms because my parents fell in love and got married. How did you end up with a mom and a dad?"
- "Some kids have two moms, some kids have two dads, some kids have stepparents . . . I just have two moms. All families are different. Families are about love."

Third, have a plan for Mother's Day and Father's Day. This is a problem not reserved for same-sex parents, as children in single-parent homes may encounter the same issues at school when they are instructed to make a gift for Mother's Day, for example.

Aside from not observing one holiday or the other, an alternative is to draw names each year and decide which parent will be celebrated on Mother's Day and which on Father's Day. According to Cook, every family is different when it comes to how or what they choose to celebrate, and ideally kids will feel comfortable owning it. To that end, Cook recommends giving children a single "this is what we do" statement that briefly explains the unique way in which their family chooses to celebrate (or not).

Another way to prepare your family is to recognize the effect of internalized homophobia, which is defined as a set of negative attitudes and effects toward homosexuality in other persons and toward homosexual features in oneself. Both internalized homophobia and experiences of outside criticism may mean that families need more time in therapy.[47]

Safe Haven vs. Secure Exploration

I want to pivot now to a major challenge for same-sex parents: how are traditional mother and father roles fulfilled?

Inge Bretherton calls out the problem. "Mothers and fathers differentiate their attachment roles such that mothers primarily address safe haven needs whereas fathers primarily support secure exploration."[48]

While generally true, I realize that not every family's mother and father behave in this way. In my own growing-up family, I could argue that my father was much more a nurturer, while my mother was the one who encouraged challenge and risk-taking. In the family that I raised, I definitely fell on the side of secure exploration, but for various reasons, there was a good mix of safe haven in my parenting as well.

How are these roles fulfilled in same-sex parenting situations? One study found that, irrespective of gay or lesbian family type, children used the primary caregiver more as a safe haven and the secondary caregiver more as a secure base for exploration, though they reported high levels of both types of support from both parents. The researchers inferred that, regardless of their gender, there remains a fundamental attachment figure who transmits their internal model of relationships to their child through parenting behavior, partly independent of the other parent's actions.[49]

An important unison parenting point is to identify each parent's style and determine how the children are given both safe haven and secure exploration.

This brings us to an important unison parenting point because it's not ideal to be independent in parenting styles without forethought. In any family, but especially in same-sex-led families, it's important to identify each parent's style and determine how the children are given both safe haven and secure exploration. This does not necessarily mean that one parent fills one role and the second parent, by default, takes the other. There may be a combination offered by each parent.

What I'm stressing here is intentionality. Parents should be aware of their style and performance and the children's needs, then intentionally address how any gaps will be filled.

Returning to the example of Meg and Sherry, Sherry's natural inclination is toward safe haven parenting. Meg, the birth mother, trends toward secure exploration, but generally speaking, they do not see a gap in how they share the roles.

An alternative I would lift up is how to use family and friends to supplement roles if the parents both trend one way or the other. "Becky" and "Brenda", another lesbian couple, moved closer to family to encourage interaction from an uncle. Later, they moved away and looked to a community of friends to help support their children, though there are no males in the group that offer support.

However they are supplied, it's vital in same-sex families to provide both roles of safe haven and secure exploration, roles typically delivered along gender lines. You can see how this same issue can affect families without both roles in the household, such as divorced situations.

Summary of Collective Parenting

Key Points

- Divorced parents should collaborate, not manipulate children.
- Parenting partners, especially in divorced/remarried situations, can shift roles over time. An example is a stepmother who transitions from friend to a parental figure.
- Stepparents can become allies for absent parents by asking for their wishes and communicating status.
- If a father is absent from the home, be open to trustworthy male role model alternatives.
- Grandparents who are parenting should seek groups that provide support and share ideas.
- Same-sex parents should prepare their children for potential bullying, criticism, and questions.

Unison Parenting Foundation

- Divorced couples should set aside personal differences to agree on and execute a parenting framework.
- Multiple parenting frameworks across blended families can cause inconsistency and confusion and be detrimental to children's needs. Counseling among parenting partners is advised to plan a common framework.
- Birth parents should consistently cede control to grandparents who are parenting the child.
- Any family with an imbalance of gender roles should determine how to provide children with both safe haven and secure exploration.
- Unison parenting techniques of proactive, reactive, adaptive, and supportive parenting are all useful in collective parenting situations.

Intermission: "Proud" Parenting Moments

This is a pretty serious book, so let's have some laughs before we get into the topic of the teen years.

I like to ridicule myself for my "proud" parenting moments. No, I'm not proud of them—these are some of my harmless but stupid mistakes that have become family lore.

Filming Austin Is Apparently like Filming Bigfoot

I somehow managed to botch it whenever it came time to record video of my middle child, Austin.

It started early. When he was five years old, Austin and Sara combined for a duet in church on Mother's Day called "A Mother's Love." I was using the bulky video camera that was common in the late twentieth century. It had a lot of great features, like infrared recording for very low light. Well, guess what it was set on for this monumental family recording? Yep, infrared.

Infrared is heat-based, so everyone came out greenish. It looked like an Army Night Ranger recording, even though the service was inside during morning hours. That's not a recording I show a lot.

Another famous incident was when Austin was slated for a solo number with the church youth choir at their annual Valentine's show. I was so proud and excited and . . . disappointed. Five seconds into his song, the video camera conked out. Dad had forgotten to charge the battery!

I got it right on another occasion—and then wrong. I did not know of a surprise Austin had for us at his middle school band concert. When the band played "Funkytown," Austin leaped out in front and did a hilarious, energetic dance. I think the band director approved the idea but did not know what Austin was going to do! It was a great moment, a crowd pleaser, a wonderful surprise, and I actually captured Austin's big moment on videotape this time!

Until I didn't. Sometime later, that tape was in the camera when Austin tried a crazy peanut butter challenge in our kitchen. I quickly grabbed the camera, thinking a different tape was inserted, and started recording him— right over "Funkytown."

So when we watch the video of "Funkytown," Austin starts dancing. Shortly, it cuts to him in our kitchen, with a mouth full of peanut butter, drooling and gurgling loudly. Then the tape returns for the finale of "Funkytown." Of all my video foibles, Austin never lets me live that one down!

Left Behind

Sara had her own proud parenting moment when Rebecca was four and the boys were in the midst of baseball season.

I was coaching Austin's team. We had left for a game. Sara was planning to take Anthony to his baseball practice, then attend the game.

In our chaotic life at the time, we didn't communicate well. Sara thought I had taken Rebecca with me. It didn't help that Rebecca was upstairs in her room, quietly coloring, as Sara and Anthony headed out the door.

When Sara showed up at the game, I met and challenged her, "Where's Rebecca?"

Sara said, "I thought you brought her to the game."

I replied, "No! I can tell you where she is. She's at Suzanne's house [our neighbor]."

Having found herself alone, Rebecca went across the street to our neighbor's house. It wasn't unusual for our kids to flow from one house to the other. She did the right thing, and our neighbor had called to alert me.

Sara drove to our neighbor's, abashed and worried, thinking she would find an emotionally scarred Rebecca. But our little girl was happily watching cartoons.

My turn to do the same happened when Rebecca was in high school. I was teaching a young adult class that met at noon after the last worship service. Rebecca would hang out in the youth area or on an upstairs sofa while I taught. Then I would text her on the way out, and she would join me at the door from wherever she was stationed.

One week, the class decided to go out for lunch at a burger joint after our lesson. Austin was visiting from college, so when we got to the burger place, I was trying to coordinate all the family orders. I knew mine and Austin's, then looked around to see what Rebecca was having and realized I had left her at the church!

I called Rebecca to tell her of my mistake and to ask for her burger order. As Austin ordered, I drove back to the church to get her. A funny side note is that I was trying to do something with my driver-side window while driving, made another mistake, and accidentally caught my left hand in the window while the automatic mechanism was raising the glass! It was actually a little dangerous, since I had to take the other hand off the wheel to lower the glass, but luckily, no one was driving near me at the time. By the way, getting your hand caught is more painful than you might think, since the mechanism is furiously trying to close the window!

Rebecca was highly insulted that I had forgotten her, but more importantly, she now had something to hold over me. Whenever I get too full of myself, she will remind me of the time that I left my daughter at church. (In fact, as I was writing this book, the anniversary of her Facebook post came around, and she made sure to forward the old post to me.)

My defense is that leaving your daughter at church is a family tradition. My parents left one of my sisters at church after her infant baptism. The extended family attended, and with all the bustle, the baby was left behind. Upon returning home, my mother realized the baby remained at church. Since my dad was the pastor, and the parsonage was next door, it only took a quick minute to run back to the sanctuary and retrieve my sleeping sister in her carrier.

Dad Sighs and Twitchy Eyes

Often, your kids know more about you than you do. That was certainly the case with two habits that I had.

The first was the "dad sigh." I would sometimes give a big sigh of disappointment when something would go wrong, and I was at the end of my rope. I wasn't aware I was doing it—until a classic case for dad sighing occurred.

I can't recall exactly where I was when I received a call from Anthony and Sara. They had traveled to a part of our metropolitan area where they hadn't been before, but where I had been numerous times. They were lost on a freeway, trying to figure out how to get back home.

I asked, "Where are you exactly?" Using the speaker phone feature, they told me their location.

Realizing they had missed their turn and were about to make it worse, I said, "Look, you've got to act quickly. Take the Carl Road exit and make a U-turn. If you miss it, you can't turn around for several miles, until you're almost to downtown Dallas."

Anthony replied, "We just drove past Carl Road while you were talking."

I let out a huge sigh and said, "OK, here's what you have to do." But they were both laughing.

I asked, "What's so funny about this?"

Anthony said, "You gave us the dad sigh."

I didn't know what they were talking about. As it turns out, I was famous in our family for my dad sighs. Sara said, "ALL of us are familiar with the dad sigh."

Most likely, the kids heard it frequently as I reviewed their grades. I exhibited an additional quirk during those Thursday grade reviews. I learned about that one after a school open house visit.

I was taking my trio of children around to see teachers at the open house when we encountered one of the math teachers. She mentioned that my kid/her student had missed a math assignment.

I said, "Oh, really?"

Upon this, the teacher looked very startled and began stammering that the assignment could be made up, so it wasn't a big deal.

My kids knew what was happening next. As soon as we had finished, and my foot hit the pavement outside the school entrance, I turned to the child in question and exclaimed, "What is going on with your math homework?"

The child replied, "I knew you were going to jump on me when I saw the eye twitch. And my teacher saw it too."

I didn't know about any eye twitch. It turns out that when I get mad, my right eye starts to twitch involuntarily. I suppose I must react like Inspector Dreyfus in the old *Pink Panther* movies, when his eye starts to spasm at the mere mention of Inspector Clouseau's name. (If those movies preceded you, you'll enjoy looking them up. There are highlight reels.)

That explains the teacher's startled reaction. I must have appeared like a maniac, ready to do my child harm!

The strange thing is that I have never been able to detect the twitching myself. During subsequent eye twitches, a kid would say, "You're doing it again, Dad." I had no idea.

I suppose it's to my advantage that my body contains involuntary parenting tools like dad sighs and twitchy eyes that made my kids sit up and take notice!

PART TWO:
PARENTING TEENS

Welcome to the Teen Years

You have watched your child grow. You have seen changes in them, their gradual growth as they age. To use a nature analogy, it seems like you have been going through rolling hills that gradually increase in height.

Suddenly, you're confronted with radical changes. You're in the mountains now. The heights are astounding. The cliffs and valleys are too. You have gone from a stroll to a brisk walk to mountain climbing.

Suddenly your child has changed, and so has the complexity of the situations they face. Whereas you spent years controlling their environment, you have lost control of their environment. Not only does the child seem less able to be controlled, but the environment is also difficult to control. Unless you put your child in isolation and home school them, you're not in control anymore. Even if you do home school, you won't control every situation.

That precious child has changed radically. Of course, the lore of parents is that their child has turned into a monster. From working with church youth for thirty-plus years, I can tell you that does happen. The opposite can happen too. Despite the growing pains of adolescence, your child can change for the better. Most actually do!

I can cite a lot of examples of monsters, and I can cite a lot of examples of radical growth. I remember a girl I'll call Beth. In her sixth and seventh grade years in youth group, I'm not sure if she said more than a few words to anyone but her closest friends. When Beth returned in the fall of her eighth-grade year, she suddenly had become a take-charge, vocal leader! It was surprising and welcome, especially because we had lost some good leaders to high school, and there was a void. By the time Beth graduated from high school, she had become one of the best leaders we ever had in youth group.

So you never know. Taking a quote from Forrest Gump's mother, teens are a box of chocolates. You never know what you're going to get from time to time as you dip into the box.

The Amoeba in Your House

One reason a teenager seems so random is that we think of them as a ginger-bread person when we should be thinking of them as an amoeba. Let me explain.

Consider your child as having five aspects or attributes to them. They are made up of physical, mental, emotional, social, and spiritual components. Here is a picture of the ideal, balanced teenager.

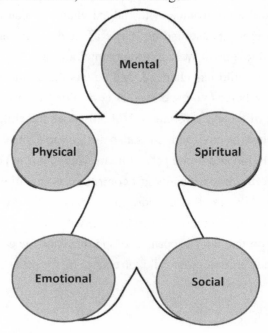

In reality, your teen looks more like an amoeba:

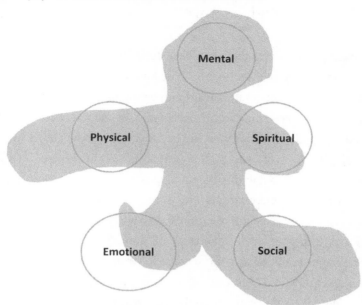

Your teen is growing in irregular, erratic ways. In some ways, they may quickly develop, perhaps physically or socially. Or maybe they are way behind the other attributes socially, emotionally, or spiritually.

Like an amoeba, these attributes can shape-shift in proportion to each other. Perhaps they level off physically, even falling behind others, but then their mental capabilities take a big leap.

The point, of course, is that they do not grow at some even, logical, proportional pace. This is why they may seem so "together," but then you find that they're an emotional wreck. Perhaps they have a close relationship with the Lord, but they have a hard time talking to anyone else.

I propose thinking of your child not as a monster but as an amoeba in order to understand them better.

Respond with Collaboration

There are a lot of ways to respond to the mountainous terrain of the teen years. Many parents become either scared or controlling, which is just another form of being scared. They simply don't know how to handle this transition.

> Many parents become either scared or controlling, which is just another form of being scared.

Moreover, parents know their own backstories, their own rebellion, their own experimentation. They fear the teen will make the same mistakes they did—or worse. So they either over-rotate toward preventing those mistakes or over-rotate toward encouraging those mistakes. Hence, you will encounter parents who want to be the cool parents and offer your kid booze at their home gatherings because "they're going to do it anyway, so they might as well do it here." It's not only damaging for them to do that; it's illegal in most, if not all, states.

You will also encounter parents who become overprotective helicopter parents who keep a strict leash on their child. I would point you back to the **Supportive Parenting** chapter and the story of Ronald in the **Dominant Parent** section. He never received any more freedom from his parents in response to his proven discipline and continued growth as a person.

I have stated all the way through the book that your parenting should change in the teen years. I propose a collaborative model instead of confrontational or acquiescent models.

Ready, Set, GOodbye

The premise of the collaborative model is a stark one: you have four years. (Assuming we're defining teens as starting in high school; in real-

ity, the teen years start in middle school. But I'll use four years to make my point.)

You have four years to finish producing an adult.

Four years to mold a teen into an adult. Four years to prepare your child to function in an adult world. Four years to use all these high school events and moments as a trial period, proving ground, and grand experiment to get them ready for adulthood.

Breathe for a moment. That is a very scary proposition!

And believe me, you have a long way to go to create that adult. But remember, your ultimate job in parenting is what? To produce an adult!

You're near a point of not only telling them, "Ready, Set, GO!" but "Ready, Set, GOodbye!"

Now, the adult creation is not yours alone by any means. In fact, God's fingerprints are all over this process, for both you and for your child. It's God's natural plan for kids to be born, to grow into adults, and to take their own place in the world, wherever and however that might be.

From the trial-and-error of raising my own kids, from observing many families and their parenting philosophies, and from interacting with the results of that parenting (the teens themselves), I am confident to tell you that the teen years don't have to be confrontational.

Instead, those years can and should be collaborative.

Ultimately, you and your child have the same goal: to grow them into an independent adult.

Ultimately, you and your child have the same goal: to grow them into an independent adult. You can't lose sight of that fact in the details of adolescence.

It's best to show them that vision as well, to make it a shared vision, to implement a system where you foster their growth with incremental decision-making during the teen years. You will be there to overrule some decisions, yes. You will be there to protect them and guide them. But you will also be there to help them with their trial decisions, to make their mistakes in a safe environment with limited consequences, and to build them to making good decisions on their own.

A great statement to counter rebellion is:

In four years (or three or two or one), you're going to get to decide all that for yourself, for the rest of your life. Until then, you're living under this framework, and we're going to follow it because I see it as the best way to bring you into independent adulthood, which we both want. It won't be long before you'll get to decide how much of it you want to follow and how much of it you'll discard.

Believe me, as much as your child wants to break away, they also are frightened by the prospect. Whenever you bring up an independent adulthood just around the corner, they are going to gulp just a little at that reality (at least on the inside).

You and your child have a shared vision of independent adulthood. You may differ on the details of how to get there. But if you take a collaborative approach, where you clearly are supportive and are acting not to control them but to grow them, then I believe you will encounter less resistance and will find a new partner: your growing child.

Although a chapter comes next on collaborative parenting techniques, the idea of collaborative parenting runs through every chapter in the teen section. Please consider my suggestions as emerging from that paradigm.

Collaborative Parenting

Meditation: Colossians 1:10–11

"So that you may live a life worthy of the Lord and please him in every way: bearing fruit in every good work, growing in the knowledge of God, being strengthened with all power according to his glorious might so that you may have great endurance and patience."

Great endurance and patience. Those are welcome qualities for parents, especially parents of teens.

Like all of life, parenthood is raw material for spiritual growth. The events of life can help us grow spiritually, or they can set us back spiritually. It's our choice to make.

Of course, we're not alone in that process. The Holy Spirit is our guide for every situation. Through the Spirit's help, we aim to live a worthy and pleasing life.

We also hope to bear the fruit of children who will join us in living a worthy and pleasing life. There are so many ways we want them to grow: spiritually, mentally, physically, emotionally, socially.

You're on quite the journey as a parent. It's a spiritual journey as well. In steady state, we want to grow in the knowledge of God and prepare well to bear fruit for His kingdom. In the difficult times, we need to lean on the might of God to pass through them.

The end result is to increase our endurance and patience. Pray for endurance and patience. Pray to keep up your focus, to withstand turmoil, to see your teen with patient eyes after having traversed those years yourself. Release your teen into God's care because you can only control and achieve so much, and the rest is left up to the Holy Spirit to finish.

How to Bring Yourself to Collaboration

After reading the introductory section on parenting teens, you may wonder how you will bring your teen to a point of collaboration. I would suggest that you must first start at the other end, preparing *yourself* to collaborate with your child.

Parents and teens are crafting a new relationship. It is not quite an adult/peer relationship, but it's certainly a step toward it. You are beginning to see your child, to a degree, as a peer.

This is a hard mindset to adopt, especially when you're experiencing this wonky amoeba that lives in your house. But it's essential to begin giving your child the respect that comes with growing maturity. Recognize where they are indeed growing; even call it out to them at the right time, to show the respect you have for them.

There are two internal issues that you must first resolve in your mind in order to collaborate with your child: giving up control and giving up pride.

Giving Up Control

To begin, I'm not suggesting that you *abandon* control. You will still need to maintain a firm parental position, using the loving and firm parenting style. But you do need to give up some control so that the teen has the right to make more choices.

Some of these choices can't be stopped. Your teen will not remain under your supervision throughout each day as much as in earlier years. However, you'll still be engaging in tug-of-war over other choices.

My point is that the biggest choice that you can't control is your teen's identity. One of the hardest phases that a parent goes through is accepting that the child must create their own identity.

Remember when your child was an infant? There was a stage, very early on, when your baby did not realize that they were a separate entity from you. By six to nine months of age, a baby begins to realize they are a separate person surrounded by their own skin. They no longer experience floating in a sea of feelings and needs, where the outside and the inside are all mixed together. They start to understand you are separate from them and may worry when they can't see or feel you nearby.[50]

In the teen years, you're entering a new phase of autonomy, in which a teen is on the path to creating their own identity or persona. They are likely not going to desire to be your clone. While we can accept that **intellectually**, it's much more difficult to accept **emotionally**.

For example, my kids weren't allowed tattoos until they were eighteen, but two of them went for tattoos shortly afterward. I had only one piece of advice for them: don't let any tattoo limit your career choices. They have abided by that wisdom, although one of my children has some extensive tattooing and continues to add to the collection. That's not a way I would ever decorate my body. Still, both see it as part of their identity and self-expression. It is interesting to hear their rationale, the meaning each tattoo holds, and their tattooing stories. As a parent, I had to emotionally give up control over something rightfully theirs, their bodies. (Let's not get into how their grandmother felt about their tattoos!)

This is yet another scenario where the Serenity Prayer becomes essential for parents: "God, give me the serenity to accept the things I cannot change, the courage to change the things I can, and the wisdom to know the difference."

I'll also insert this nugget of insight from advice columnist Carolyn Hax: "I've come to believe the ability to think before speaking is a superpower for any parent of teens."[51]

Giving Up Pride

In the **Adaptive Parenting** chapter of the **Fundamentals** section, I discussed how your child is not your mirror. I talked about how there's a danger in seeing your child as a reflection of yourself.

Here we need to also see this tendency as a spiritual issue involving pride. C. S. Lewis, in his book *Mere Christianity*, labels pride as "The Great Sin." According to Lewis, pride or self-conceit is the utmost evil; he says it was through pride that Satan became the devil.

Note that this kind of pride is not the same as saying or feeling that you're proud of your child. It's also not when you are open to praise or even seeking praise. Rather, this kind of pride falls under the sin of comparison or competitiveness. It is the problem of thinking you are better than others and wanting to feel this or demonstrate this in some way.[52] That way may be through your child's identity and how it impacts yours.

If we exhibit this kind of pride, there are some harsh questions to ask ourselves:

- Is it not pride if we feel that we have to control our child's identity because of how it will reflect on us?
- Are we not taking something special away from them because of how it suits us?
- Are we not saying that they are inferior copies of ourselves?

In short, parenting pridefulness is a spiritual issue involving our lack of humility and our treatment of others.

As you can imagine, this is an area that requires a unison parenting viewpoint. Parenting partners must be on board with the principle of collaborative parenting. Each must examine themselves for issues of control and pride—and call out these issues in each other, if necessary.

Once you have prepared yourselves, you're ready to bring a collaboration approach to your teen.

How to Bring Your Teen into Collaboration

As you prepare to present to your teen this new relationship based on collaboration, it's important to revisit your assumptions about your teen and their willingness to function within a collaborative model. A helpful thought is to take a positive view as expressed by a method called Collaborative Problem Solving® (CPS), developed by Massachusetts General Hospital, regarded by some as the top psychiatric hospital in the United States.

CPS starts with two foundational principles:

- Teens do well if they can.
- Skill not will.

The first principle relates to a general principle that a former boss of mine used to express: no one wakes up intending to do a bad job. Teens are no different. They don't wake up each day with the goal of being challenging, with the goal of lying and manipulating, or with the goal of seeing how they can further ruin their life relationships.[53]

Teens may be limited by factors like:

- Depression.
- Anxiety.
- Trauma/PTSD.
- ADHD/ADD.[54]

The second principle considers another factor that limits teens: they may simply not have the skill to do what is asked. But parents tend to think nonconformance is due to will, not skill.

This is a very important point, and one I struggled with practically from the birth of my children. Too often, when observing noncompliance, I first thought that my child was acting out of will, out of rebellion. Certainly, that happened at times, but not as often as I assumed, as I can now see in retrospect.

If you begin, like I did, thinking the child is rebelling against you, your defenses immediately rise, your anxiety and anger rise, your common sense lowers, and your interpretative powers lower. You begin to see every statement in the context of will, not skill, and you don't listen as well. Predictably, this either leads to arguments or to harshness on the part of the parent, damaging the child's psyche.

With practice, I got better at this. With Anthony, the eldest, getting him into a car seat as a preschooler became a test of wills. With Austin, the next one, I had grown up enough to have an unemotional attitude of "I know, dude, but you have to get in the seat. Let's snap the buckle." Much more matter-of-fact.

I originally realized this positive view of teens more effectively as a youth counselor than I did as a parent. When you take yourself out of the emotional mix, and you're just listening to the teen talk when they are not "yours," you truly get a different perspective on how they feel and behave. Such experiences allowed me to understand and manage my own children better.

Again, a unison parenting point is that parenting partners need to agree to this mindset of seeing the teen in a more favorable light. It's a hard conversion because on the surface, your teen may seem more rebellious than incapable. But remember the amoeba and the imbalance of capabilities.

The Revelation of Incremental Decision-Making

As you approach your teen about the next few years, it's good to start with acknowledging their advancing status according to the process of incremental decision-making that I described in the **Adaptive Parenting** chapter of the **Fundamentals** section, in the **Ages Twelve to Eighteen** subsection; I'll repeat some of the points here. Your approach should include the following key messages:

- **You are growing up and are able to make more decisions on your own.** We (or I, when there is only one parent) acknowledge this and have been expecting this and are glad to reach this point.
- The plan all along has been to **give you more latitude and experience at making decisions.** *(If you are a recent convert to this plan, reword appropriately to say this is the plan now.)*
- As your parents, **we will modify the way we've managed the Choices Chart** and use similar yet new techniques for establishing rules and consequences.
- These rules and consequences give you **boundaries primarily for protection, not control.** Everything we're doing is primarily aimed at enabling you to make the best decisions possible when you become an adult in a few years.
- Speaking of consequences, while we will come together on assigned consequences as with the Choices Chart, there is an important caveat: **We cannot give you consequences bigger than life will give you.**
    - If you drive drunk or recklessly, or if you otherwise break the law, you'll get to encounter the justice system and possibly go to jail.
    - If you cause a pregnancy to happen, you'll have to deal with big decisions about becoming a parent.
    - If you do not study or work hard, your college and work options will become limited.
    - If you aren't careful in whatever you're doing, someone, including you, could die.
    - **No amount of parental grounding can match the realities of what life can do to you now if you misbehave.**

These last few sub-bullets are exactly why you as a parent are continuing to work with your child, giving them limits, loving them through their mistakes, teaching them, and refining their decision-making.

Don't forget the key sentence: "You have four years to become an adult."

Don't forget the key sentence: "You have four years to become an adult." (Or however much time is left.)

When talking through this with your child, I recommend you also introduce two techniques to implement in this new collaboration. They are contracts and the Collaborative Problem Solving process.

Contracts Replace Choices Chart

Let me precede everything I'm about to say with this caveat regarding replacement of the Choices Chart: If you are in a multichild family with a large age range, you may need to hold the eldest to some aspects of the family Choices Chart for continuity between siblings. However, you may have to make alterations and explanations in the Choices Chart as follows:

- The eldest may have additional or different rules and consequences.
- The eldest may have some rules and consequences that are captured in contracts rather than in the Choices Chart.
- Any differences are to respect the age differences of everyone involved, acknowledging age-appropriate behavior, privileges, and responsibilities.

In our family, because of the age span, we followed this model. Only in extreme circumstances did we use anything that looked like a contract. (Of course, the Choices Chart is a type of contract itself.)

However, I have recommended the use of contracts in my parenting classes, and I know families that have used them effectively and reported success.

I got the idea of contracts from Gary Smalley. His family used them to govern dating privileges and driving privileges.

The Smalley dating contract included the following provisions:

- The child's **character** is considered in being allowed to date. For example, if the child is caught lying, dating privileges are suspended for a time.
- Each **dating situation** is evaluated separately, but well-organized, school-sponsored activities are favored.
- Every member of the family must **approve the dating partner**, reflecting a close-knit family concerned about the well-being of all.
- The **curfew** would vary depending on character traits and trust-worthiness.[55]

Let me add a few comments about how our family implemented dating rules.

- Once a teen wanted to date someone, they had to notify us of the new relationship and the transition from friend to date. This is because we had a different curfew and different rules for going out with a group of friends (who might be mixed gender) compared to a dating scenario. Yes, violations of this policy occurred, but we caught on and challenged the teen for not informing us of the change.
- We parents had to meet the dating party before dating was approved.
- Originally, dating was confined to school, family, and church activities, and expanded as time went on.
- If a dating partner was brought home, you could be in your bedroom with them, but only with the door open. Siblings and parents were free to enter. (And did—on occasion, I sent a younger sibling to wander through the room for some reason.)

- BIG RULE: This applied not only to dating but to all situations involving someone else's house—a parent had to be present at the house. Teens were not to be alone in the house. As we'll discuss later, this is not a foolproof policy, as the other parents might (and did) look the other way more than we desired or might decide to leave while our child was present—despite conversations we had with them about our policy.

Driving contracts are becoming more and more common. You can find samples online, so I won't spend much space here except to cite the principles we used.

- Driving is indeed a *privilege*. One must be mature to be a driver because lives are at stake. Therefore, a teen could not begin driving until they showed maturity and followed well other rules of the house. Driving privileges could be (and were) taken away for maturity violations. These included traffic violations and poor scholastic performance.
- Driving isn't only a privilege, but a family responsibility. If you're allowed to drive, you're also required on occasion to drive on behalf of the family, such as taking a younger sibling to practice.
- After receiving their license, the teen driver went through stages of how many non-family-members could be in the car with them. At first, no one. Then one person could. Then you could fill up the car with legal seating.
- To take someone else home required permission. Over time, this restriction was lifted for common, recurring situations.
- One of the big phrases I used (and you'll hear again in the **Preventative Parenting** chapter): There is no "blank check." You must tell us where you're going, you must be at the place or places we agreed upon, and you have a defined time to be home.

I want to emphasize that dating and driving contracts are clearly a unison parenting consideration. Parenting partners must align on the rules first before approaching the teen to establish a contract or policy, presenting a unified front, and only allowing amendments if each parenting partner agrees.

Try Collaborative Problem Solving

Let's delve further into an aforementioned technique for reconciling behavioral issues. I am suggesting bringing them into a collaboration by treating teens more like equals.

Collaborative Problem Solving®, or CPS, from Thinkkids.org, part of Massachusetts General Hospital, is not innovative. Other sources have recommended such techniques for adult or business interactions. To me, the difference is in applying the principles to teens and children, usually for kids with challenging behavior. I feel CPS is a good method to treat your teen as a fledgling adult.

Building upon the principles that kids do as well as they can, and skill is the issue rather than will, the process begins with identifying triggers to a child's challenging behavior and the specific skills they need help developing. The next step involves partnering with the child to build those skills and develop lasting solutions to problems that work for everyone.[56]

CPS steps in contentious situations are:

- Empathy and seek to understand
- Seek to be understood
- Collaborate on solutions to the problem[57]

The first step is to meet with your teen and seek to understand from their perspective and what they need. This is not a time to counterargue or to provide facts or evidence, but to simply listen to understand where they are coming from. It may not be rational. It may not be true. But, when your teen feels that you totally understand where they are coming from, they are more likely to listen to you and where you are coming from.

If you can put aside your own emotions, not interrupt or interject, and listen to understand, your teen's more likely to listen when you talk. Asking clarifying questions with the intent to understand better is important.[58]

This reminds me of techniques from a model called Crucial Conversations. To succeed in crucial conversations, we must really care about the interests of others—not just our own.[59]

After hearing out the teen, the second step is to flip the roles and present your side of the story. Remember that the teen may not be as good at listening as you are; they may be developing the skill as you speak. You may have to remind them that you listened to them, and they owe you the same respect in return.

The third step is to collaborate on solutions to the problem. This step reminds me of two things.

First, reactive parenting scenarios. I recommended in that chapter to huddle together as parents to decide on consequences in unusual situations. Another approach is to collaborate with the teen, helping them realize the ramifications of their actions and asking them for input on what consequences they should face. (In proactive parenting scenarios, governed by Choices Chart or contracts, the consequences would already be known.)

A reminder of the long-term mutual purpose of raising them to make good adult decisions is a good starting point.

Second, Crucial Conversations techniques use an approach called *mutual purpose*. I feel this approach would be more appropriate to a scenario such as the teen wanting more freedom (going to a concert, curfew) but the parents wanting to retain limits. Since you want to align with the teen on the long-term mutual purpose of raising them to make good adult decisions, the reminder of that mutual purpose is a good starting point. Then you can address the scenario in front of you from the perspective of joining forces in searching for a solution that serves everyone.[60]

A safe way to move this from a negotiation to a collaborative approach is to use brainstorming to come up with alternatives. Brainstorming doesn't mean you even agree with the alternative you submit; you're just generating ideas, often in hopes of discovering a solution that isn't apparent at first.

A final thought is to remember that both you and your teen may be treading new ground. CPS may be one of their first attempts at behaving like an adult. For parents, it might feel different to bring their child into a more equitable position in discussions. A little grace is nice for everyone involved.

Adaptive Parenting Model to Grow Decision-Making

I want to rev up the discussion on how to grow decision-making in your teen. We have covered the stages of incremental decision-making, giving an overview of what that looks like. Now I will show a more detailed way to grow your teen's decision-making to adulthood.

I'll admit that this model looks pretty complex. I hope it will seem a lot simpler once I explain it.

Its purpose is threefold:

- Help to grow your child's ability to operate independently.
- Gradually teach them a methodology for problem-solving.
- Determine what stage they are in and your resulting actions by how your child behaves and what they tell you.

The starting point is a well-known business leadership model called Situational Leadership,[61] based on a book by leadership experts Paul Hersey and Ken Blanchard. The model describes four leadership styles a manager can use based on the capabilities, willingness, and confidence of the employee. For my purposes, I've adapted the model to parenting and tacked on a couple of layers that I used in managing employees, also adapted for parenting, in order to specifically grow their decision-making capabilities.

The first layer of adaptive parenting looks a lot like the Situational Leadership model. Let me reveal the model quadrant by quadrant. (Diagrams start in the following section on scenario descriptions.)

We start in the lower right with the child who has a low level of ability and low level of confidence or willingness. The child's capabilities will ascend as we move through the model in a counterclockwise fashion, ending at the lower left with the child who is most capable and confident.

The words *Tell*, etc., indicate your action in dealing with a child at their level.

It's important to note that your child may be in different stages for different parts of their life. For example, perhaps the child has learned how to be handy around the house, gaining knowledge and experience on how to perform various tasks. They might be farther around on the curve. Then they begin learning to drive, and suddenly, in that part of their life, they are stationed in the lower right quadrant, still learning and not very confident yet.

Therefore, I will speak in terms of tasks that the child faces as a generic way to cover a particular aspect of their life. The goal, of course, is to grow their capabilities so that they move around the rectangle toward the optimal quadrant of Delegation.

Adaptive Parenting Model Scenario Descriptions
Let's walk through each quadrant to describe it further.

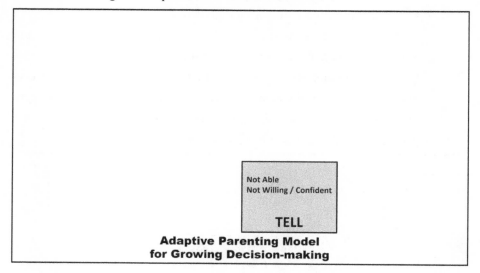

1. Tell
   - Child is not able or equipped for a given task.
   - Child is also not willing or confident to do the task.

This is the style to use for a child that is a novice or less capable in relation to the task. You basically tell them what to do in detail, and then they execute the task.

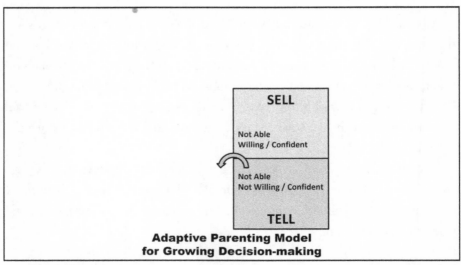

**Adaptive Parenting Model
for Growing Decision-making**

2. Sell
   - Child is not able or equipped for a given task.
   - Child is willing and confident to do the task.

This is a style to use when the child has become more confident, but you don't completely trust their capabilities yet. In this case, they may be more opinionated on how to do the task; their confidence is growing, but their capability hasn't grown as much. You'll have to sell them on the idea of doing a task a particular way, so you can expect some persuasion and negotiation to take place.

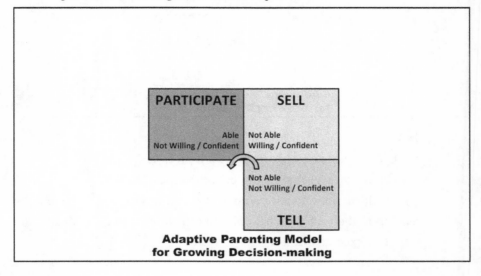

**Adaptive Parenting Model
for Growing Decision-making**

3. Participate
   - Child is able and equipped for a given task.
   - Child is not willing or confident to do the task.

   At this point, you're dealing with a child that is becoming more capable and effective but doesn't think they can fly on their own without your help. You assign more responsibility to this child, but you still insert yourself in the process to answer their questions and give final approval.

   For many people, it is hard to go beyond this step. They don't have the confidence to take on more responsibility; sometimes they are unwilling to take on more responsibility. You become more of a cheerleader and a sounding board in this stage.

Sometimes you have to implement parental tough love, withdrawing in order for them to take charge.

Sometimes you have to implement parental tough love. You intentionally withdraw as much as possible in order for them to take charge, then you evaluate with them how things went.

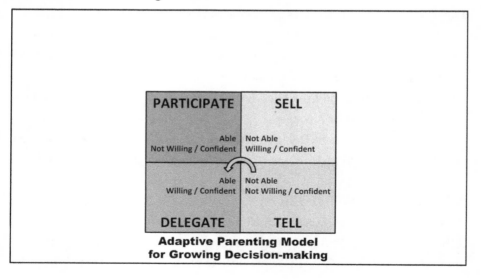

**Adaptive Parenting Model
for Growing Decision-making**

4. Delegate
- Child is able and equipped for a given task.
- Child is willing and confident to do the task.

    Ah, this is a beautiful land, where a capable, confident, proactive teen handles projects effectively with minimal guidance and interaction! At this level, you can delegate to your child and need to interact very little on decisions. All you need to do is to monitor their progress occasionally or even just learn the result when complete.

Application of Four Quadrants

Let me give an example of how the adaptive parenting model to grow decision-making would work in practice, using the example of cooking.

Your child starts as a novice in the kitchen, at the **Tell** level. When teaching them to cook, you assign less complex tasks to them. You safeguard the child and direct all actions.

At the **Sell** level, your child may become more confident and will want to experiment; however, their ability is still limited. You need to persuade them what is right. Govern their experimentation, allowing for low-risk failure and consequences. Keep things safe, but if a dish tastes bad as a result of their actions, such as if they insist on adding too much salt, it becomes a low-consequence learning event.

The next level is **Participate**. The child's ability is growing, and many tasks have been mastered. But they're not yet confident that they can pull together a more complex meal on their own. You would remain in the kitchen with them as a helper, advisor, cheerleader, and safety net, but encourage them to be the main driver of the meal.

Finally, you're able to **Delegate**. Ask them to make dinner! Or even better yet, they volunteer to make dinner tonight! It happens, and it's wonderful.

Solutions Orientation

Now let me add another layer to the picture—the problem-solving layer. Let's face it: "adulting" often means problem-solving. Adults may get tired of solving problems, but that's life, isn't it? Life presents one problem after another. Those who can develop a solutions orientation to solving problems can successfully adult.

What do I mean by solutions orientation? This is the opposite of whining about a problem or procrastinating or ignoring a problem. A person with a solutions orientation accepts that a problem has occurred that they must address, then takes reasonable, well-timed steps toward solving the problem.

Ideally, you want to develop your teen into someone who can do the following:

- Understand and articulate the problem they're facing.
- Identify alternative solutions. They are able to identify multiple alternatives, not just the first one they think of.
- Correctly rank the alternatives from best to worst.
- Choose the right solution.
- Proactively implement the right solution.

Here are how those capabilities map onto the adaptive parenting model to grow decision-making that I have so far explained.

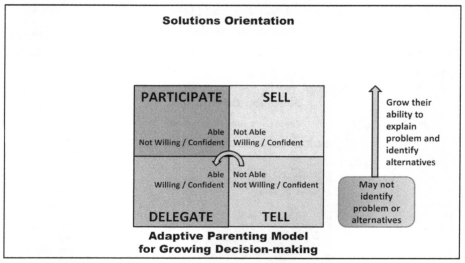

At the **Tell** level, the child is too inexperienced to identify solutions to problems; in fact, they may not even be able to clarify the problem or identify possible solution alternatives. This goes along with them not being able and

not being confident. So at this level, you want to grow their ability to identify
and explain problems and solution alternatives.

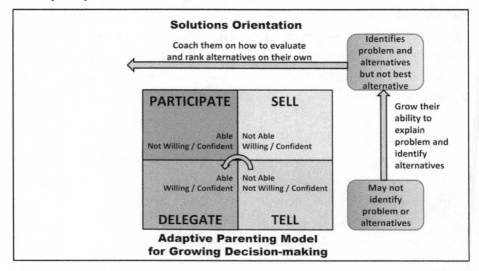

At the **Sell** level, the child can identify problems and alternatives but not
the best alternative. They're more willing and confident to make a decision and
go with it, but they are not yet able to select the best alternative. So they make
wrong decisions. Here you want to coach them to evaluate and rank alternatives, and to understand pros and cons of each possible solution. Show them a
structured way to select the best solutions to problems.

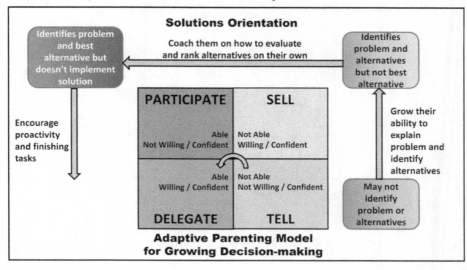

At the **Participate** level, the child can identify problems and the best alternative but may have difficulty in carrying things forward and implementing a solution. It's either a motivation problem of not being willing or a confidence problem. At this level, you may need to push them, encouraging proactivity and finishing tasks. This is a time when you may be focusing on their organizational skills, getting them to focus, or not allowing them to procrastinate because they are uncomfortable with their ability to follow through.

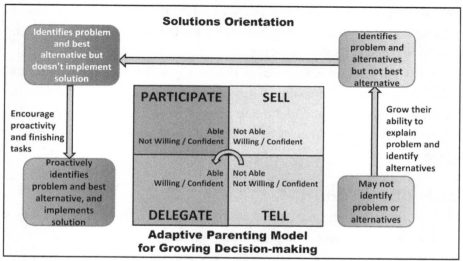

Once the child has mastered themselves, they arrive at the **Delegate** level: capable, willing, confident, and able to proactively identify problems and alternatives, select the best alternative, and implement the solution to the finish line.

Application of Solutions Orientation

Let me give an example from our daughter Rebecca's gymnastics career. She had participated for several years and was having a lot of success, though as she was entering seventh grade and as her body was maturing from childhood, it was getting harder for her to execute advanced moves. She wasn't scoring as well in meets.

More importantly, Rebecca was starting to realize that she was much more than a gymnast. The amount of time she was putting into gymnastics was less worthwhile now, as she had more options in her life as a middle schooler.

Now at this point, these were vague feelings. I started helping Rebecca to consider the day she would move on from gymnastics.

It took about a year to help her along the path of identifying the problem better and examining alternatives. As Rebecca was winding up seventh grade and thinking about her eighth-grade year, suddenly she was in a position to race through these last stages of identifying the problem, the alternatives, and how to implement them without my help.

Next thing I know, Rebecca was posting on Facebook her nine reasons for quitting gymnastics. They were well-thought out and mature, and it was clear that she had made a decision and wasn't looking back. I was as proud of her that day as I was of anything she accomplished in gymnastics.

Stuck or Streaming

Before I introduce the final piece of the model, I realize the model seems more cluttered and more complex. At the same time, I hope you can see the advantages and are able to use it. One key point is that you now have two ways to identify where your child is in their decision-making development in a given area.

1. First, you can assess how able they are and how willing or confident they are. Those are the inner boxes we started with.
2. Second, you may pick up on their development in how they look at problems and alternative solutions. Those are the outer arrows and boxes.

I have one final overlay, a technique called Stuck or Streaming. You may use this technique in all four stages, but you'll find it especially useful in the final two stages.

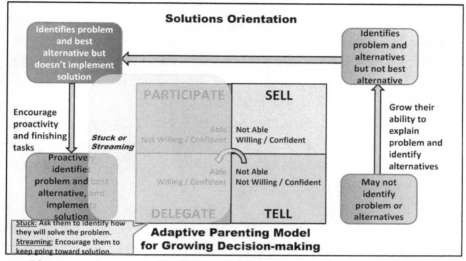

Please see the rounded light gray Stuck or Streaming box that overlays the Participate and Delegate boxes.

> Stuck or Streaming is useful in counseling or listening to anyone who is weighing how to solve a problem.

Stuck or Streaming[d] is a method that is useful in parenting, marriage, business, or practically any endeavor in which you communicate with people. In some cases, you will be in a parent or supervisor role. In some cases, you might be a peer or a friend. This technique is extremely useful in counseling or listening to anyone who is weighing how to solve a problem.

Stuck or Streaming gives you a way to identify where the person is in their problem-solving process, while also relieving you of any burden to fix the problem for them. This is useful when supervising people in business, to keep them from adding to your workload by making their problem *your* problem. As you can imagine, this is also useful as a parent, so that you do not take control of your children's problems when they complain to you;

---

d   I learned this technique from proprietary management training at one of my employers. I do not know whether the company found this idea from an outside source or whether it originated the idea. I have not been able to find an online reference to Stuck or Streaming as a management technique.

instead, you are able to send them back out one way or another to solve the problem themselves.

Here is what it sounds like when someone is stuck. They'll say things like:

- I really don't know what to do next.
- I thought this idea would be the answer, but it's not working out.
- I'm fresh out of ideas.
- I keep trying this plan, and I'm working so hard, but it feels like I'm getting nowhere.

And here's what you do, and it's very important because this is the point where you are tempted to solve the problem yourself. **Ask *them* how they're going to solve the problem!**

- Encourage them to reframe the problem.
- Suggest where they can go for advice (a person, an Internet source, a help site, etc.).
- Give them ideas but not solutions: "You might explore this . . ."
- Propose identifying and ranking alternatives, following the solutions orientation method from earlier.
- Encourage them to think creatively. The best boss I ever had said, "There is always an alternative. We may not like the alternative, but there is always an alternative." This gave me confidence that I could find a way.

One time, I had an employee enter my cubicle who was stuck. She was working in a technical area where I had little expertise, so I didn't know the answer to her problem. But I suggested some of the methods above for her to move forward.

After she left, the young manager in the next cube rushed into my cube. "Now I know why I'm failing as a manager!" he exclaimed. "I actually know the answer to that problem, and I would've given it to her. But I can see that in letting her solve the problem, and not taking it over myself, it's going to make her better."

Let's turn to streaming. This is when someone is actually on the path to solving their problem, but they may not realize it yet. They'll say things like:

- My project has gone well so far, but I'm worried about the next phase. I think I have a good plan, but I'm just not sure.
- I had this problem, but I think I solved it. And then this other problem cropped up, but I think I have it under control too.
- Here are the alternatives I have thought of, and I am leaning toward the third alternative as the right one. But I was wondering what you thought about it.

When you're listening to comments like these, realize that there is really nothing for you to solve here. The person is actually going in the right direction, but they're just streaming—in other words, spilling their situation, looking for confidence or even a blessing from you. Sometimes they're seeking someone else to make the decision so the weight isn't on them; that's another path you should resist.

Your response to the streamer is to congratulate them on what they've done so far and encourage them to keep on their path. Can you see that they are doing the right thing, but they're not confident in themselves? The main message is "Go forward."

Application of All Three Layers of the Model

To conclude this presentation of the adaptive parenting model to grow decision-making, let me give you an example from my parenting of my son Austin. What I want you to identify from my story is, What quadrant did I think Austin was in? Tell, Sell, Participate, or Delegate? And why did I do what I did?

Austin was a senior in high school. He wanted to attend his dream school, the big state university, but was unlikely to be accepted. However, they had a special program where you could go to a satellite state school for a year, and if you got good enough grades for certain courses, they would allow you to transfer to the main university as a sophomore. It was actually more complicated than I'm putting it because there were all kinds of rules about which courses would transfer, etc.

I had studied the program and knew most of the answers. Austin came to me, sounding stuck, asking for me to guide him on this project. But I surprised him.

- What I said was: "I'm not going to do all the investigation and decision-making for you. You're going to do it. And you can review it with me."
- What Austin heard was: "You're on your own." Which wasn't truly the case, but that's what he perceived.
- The reality? I was trying to get him to drive the investigation of alternatives, but I wanted to be involved, and was very involved, in the aspect of transfer credits because that factored into how long he would stay at the dream school and how much money he and I would need to pay over the next few years.

Now, return to the Stuck or Streaming diagram above. Which quadrant did I think he was in, and how did I address his situation accordingly?

Before I give the answer:

- Austin was able to do the task but was not confident.
- I wanted to encourage him to be proactive and drive toward a solution.
- I was with him in the kitchen, so to speak, more than he realized, but I was getting him to do the work.
- Finally, I used Stuck or Streaming techniques when he came to me with questions or issues.

So Austin was in the Participating quadrant.

What was the result? Besides getting through that event, Austin grew into the Delegating quadrant. Two years later, he decided to buy a car with his own money. He did the research on the best car for him, found a great deal, and had to act decisively because the seller was moving out of the country. He asked me for help to review the paperwork process with him. By then, he was making great decisions on his own.

A side story on this event: The seller actually had multiple potential buyers, and Austin wasn't the top bidder. He chose Austin because he said he saw the great relationship that we had as father and son, and it reminded him of his relationship with his dad. He felt like Austin would take the best care of the car he was selling.

Unison Parenting Pointers on the Model

Since this is a book on unison parenting, let me pivot back to show how important unison parenting is when implementing the adaptive parenting model to grow decision-making.

First, it's important for parenting partners to embrace the model. This doesn't mean that they are necessarily both skilled at it; perhaps it will come naturally to one or the other. But they need to both embrace the ideas of how to grow the teen's capabilities and problem-solving skills. It would undermine the process for one parent to follow the model, then for the other parent to simply solve all the problems for the teen.

Second, similar to when parents stayed aligned on the child's changes as discussed in the **Adaptive Parenting** chapter, parenting partners need to understand the quadrant in which the teen is located.

This is made more difficult by the amoeba effect. As an example, a teen may be skilled in the classroom and make great, advanced decisions there, but be unskilled socially. In this case, the teen actually operates under two different versions of the model, so parenting partners should see this together and adapt their parenting styles according to the model.

Third, the parents should remember to continue using the loving and firm parenting style in the midst of coaching problem-solving and solutions orientation. Even if you're not solving problems for the teen, you can still give love, encouragement, and support. You can help them express frustrations and sympathize with them. You can continue to watch for any acting-out behaviors and make sure that limits are still in place and enforced.

The Resistant Teen

Now that you have an understanding of the plan for collaborative parenting, let's talk about the monkey wrench that can gum up the machinery: your teen.

Despite your best efforts, your teen could be resistant to collaborating with you. Let me address the most likely ways this can happen, in descending order of likelihood and ascending order of difficulty.

Distrust

It's natural that a teen could be skeptical of a collaborating parent. Your behavior might be a big change from what they have previously seen. Your new plan could be unclear or difficult to accept. But most likely, it's the age-old problem of simple distrust between parent and child.

I once created a video on this topic for my church parenting classes. In it, I emphasized the different commitments that parents were making to the teen, and I asked for the teen to commit to only one thing: trust.

For the distrustful teen, you should ask for the same, perhaps in these words:

> *Please trust that my actions are motivated by what I have told you and that I am doing the best I can to help you become a capable adult.*
> *Please trust that I am not playing power games with you. Instead, I am taking a long view while balancing that with the day-to-day activities of your teen years.*
> *Please trust that I am basing my approach on a successful parenting model and not just making up stuff as I go along.*
> *Please trust that I truly have your best interests at heart and am partnering with you, step by step, toward the mutual goal of making your own great decisions as you reach adulthood.*

I have seen parents who are able to win over their teens and build good relationships, not so much by these words above, but by their sincerity, by their open conversation, by their apologies, and by their time invested in their children.

> Parents are able to win over their teens by their sincerity, by their open conversation, by their apologies, and by their time invested in their children.

There's an old saying that up until age ten to twelve, children—by their actions—are saying, "Look at me." After that, they want you to know: "Listen to me." The listening and speaking techniques discussed earlier in this chapter are essential for addressing distrust.

It's important to know that, just as a teen can quickly lose trust with you that takes time to rebuild, you can also lose trust with your teen and face an uphill battle to regain it. If you do slip up and get outside of the collaborative parenting model with trust-breaking results, you will need to own that mistake. Apologize to your teen. Admit that you fell into a bad habit. Affirm that you really want to collaborate with them. Ask for them to give you a chance to rebuild trust through your upcoming actions.

To proactively prevent loss of trust, ask directly for your child to monitor you and let you know if they sense you wandering from the collaborative approach. For example, let's say that you come down hard on their mistake and assign a consequence that seems harsh. It would be best to stay within the bounds of your contracts with them, but still, there may be reasons (see the **Reactive Parenting** chapter as a reminder).

In this case, it would be good to talk it out. Explain why you selected this consequence. Offer a path to rebuild trust with you, as was done by Brie's parents in the **Reactive Parenting** chapter. Hear the teen out for what might be considered unfair consequences and be open to modifying such consequences.

Stubbornness

Some people just have to do things their own way. That's how they learn. They have to convince themselves of a particular way to do things based on experience, not by what someone told them.

In some respects, this is an admirable trait. A teen with that attitude is not likely to join a cult, for example. But they can be frustrating to train!

I recall a young man named "Rusty." Rusty would go out and do things his own way, no matter what his parents would tell him or warn him about. It wasn't unusual for his way to lead to the calamity about which his parents cautioned. Rusty would admit to his parents that their way was right, then immediately head out and go his own way on another topic where he disagreed with his parents.

While this was frustrating for his parents, they had to pray a lot and rely on Proverbs 22:6, that a child will eventually return to his parents' ways.

The stubborn teen requires the techniques mentioned in the Sell quadrant. You will have to negotiate and navigate differences with this child. Do your best to place any guardrails you can to reduce the consequences of their actions, and allow certain behaviors while drawing the best line you can on others.

Stubbornness is listening to you and deciding not to take your advice. Rebellion is when they don't listen to you anymore.

A key unison parenting point is for parents to recognize and agree whether the teen is being stubborn or rebellious. Those are two different things that I would summarize like this: Stubbornness is listening to you and deciding not to take your advice. Rebellion is when they don't listen to you anymore.

Rebellion

Open rebellion is difficult to deal with and painful to watch. Your child completely rejects your viewpoint and perhaps even societal norms or laws in order to act according to their will or by the influence of someone else that does not share your values.

To comprehensively deal with this issue goes beyond the scope of this book because there is no simple answer, and you may be encountering a tumultuous lifelong

situation. I know parents, siblings, and even children who have experienced such situations with family members. Their experiences remind me again of how messy love can be.

Thus, I would recommend turning to other resources to address full-on rebellion and misbehavior that can extend into the adult years. However, I do have ideas to share with you.

As I've written before and will write again, a mantra to insert into the teen's head is that "Life will give you bigger consequences than I can." This is a great summation, but it does contain more details to point out to the teen.

- Not only does life assign bigger consequences than I can, but I cannot protect you from those consequences. If you choose such rebellion, you will experience consequences where we can only support you from a distance. (For example, that distance might be the thickness of the glass in the prison conversation room.)
- Depending on the nature of the rebellion, you may affect other people's lives in substantial ways. Depending on the situation, you will owe something to them as a result, a debt you didn't plan on and that constrains you going forward.
- You seek freedom and options, but bad choices can remove your freedom and your options. That's a simple fact of life, not my rule.

Remind them that they can turn around and choose another direction. Call on their spiritual training (which, unfortunately, they may no longer value), reminding them that God offers fresh starts for the repentant. Ask them to adhere to the family values with which they were raised.

This is a time when one of my recommendations later in the book can come in handy. Ideally, there will be other influential people in the teen's life that might get such points across better than you. Trust me, as a youth counselor, I discovered time after time that I could give the same message to the teen as their parents had, but they reacted differently when it came from me. While that was frustrating for parents to discover, they were grateful that there was a spiritual guide speaking truth into their child's life.

This has been a chapter largely about collaborating and teaching. As I just indicated, one of the most important teaching areas is spirituality. We want our teens to own their faith and make good spiritual decisions in the teen years and beyond. I call this process formative parenting, and it's the subject of the next chapter.

Summary of Collaborative Parenting

Key Points

- You have four years to produce an adult together.
- Collaborating requires giving up excessive parental control and pride.
- Increment the teen's decision-making scope while protecting trial decisions with boundaries.
- Use contracts to govern teen situations like dating and driving.
- Collaboration involves listening and creating solutions together. Focus on mutual purpose.
- Use the adaptive parenting model to grow decision-making to help the teen and to understand how best to manage them as parents.
- Ask for trust from your teen. Quickly repair your breach of any trust.

Unison Parenting Foundation

- Basic but hard: parenting partners must agree to collaborate.
- Parents must agree on how to convert from the Choices Chart to contracts, especially when younger siblings are present in the home.
- Embrace the adaptive parenting model. Adjust style together as the teen moves through skill quadrants.
- Determine together if a resistant teen is mistrusting, stubborn, or rebellious.

Formative Parenting

Meditation: Deuteronomy 6:6–9

"These commandments that I give you today are to be on your hearts. Impress them on your children. Talk about them when you sit at home and when you walk along the road, when you lie down and when you get up. Tie them as symbols on your hands and bind them on your foreheads. Write them on the door-frames of your houses and on your gates."

My preacher dad used to say that it took a child ten years of church attendance to catch on to what worship is all about. You can start the clock at any time, but it still takes ten years. Start them as an infant, and they'll understand by age ten. From a starting point of age six, they'll come around by age sixteen. If you start them at age thirteen, well, you probably won't see the results while they're in your household, assuming they'll keep going to church.

I don't know if my dad was right, but I didn't take a chance. I placed my kids in church worship services from the earliest time possible.

There were adventures and misadventures at times. We usually sat near the front row where they could see and participate. It takes some moxie to do that, I'll tell you, especially when I needed to remove one from the service for some reason. But sitting up front emphasized our commitment to worship.

Spiritual formation is essential for the child and incumbent on the parent. We want to train their young minds to be grounded in Christian principles and to love God. Maybe we're not writing the symbols on their foreheads, but we hope we're imprinting them just behind their foreheads!

Even though this chapter is about the last stages of parental obligation for spiritual formation during the teen years, it's never too early to begin building a spiritual foundation. I recall a former member of my parenting class making a guest appearance to speak to my current class. He offered this wise comment: "Many parents think they will put their child into church for a year or so to give them a religious foundation. I say, if it's only for a year, that's not much of a foundation!"

Moses told the Hebrews in Deuteronomy that as they reached the promised land, they should emphasize the Lord's decrees and commands with their children. The first such command he cites is "Love the Lord your God with all your heart and with all your soul and with all your strength." Moses then immediately proclaims the verses written above.

May we follow Moses's instruction and instill the love of the Lord foremost in our children's hearts.

Driver Training, Disciple Training

How do you teach a child to swim? Do you just throw them in the pool and shout, "Swim!"?

How do you teach your teen to drive? Do you just toss them the keys and say, "Drive!"?

How do you teach your child to be a disciple of Christ? Do you just launch a Bible in their direction and say, "Believe!"?

And do you simply drop them off at church and arrange a time to pick them up, while you go to brunch or grab a coffee or return to sleep?

I'm going to take a different approach to this chapter. As I taught parenting classes in my home church, it finally struck me that there are many similarities between driver training and disciple training. In this chapter, I will describe how you teach a teen to drive and compare those methods to how you teach a child to become a disciple.

Hopefully you began this process early in their lives, introducing them to church and Sunday school, giving them a Bible and reading from it, teaching them Christian principles—such as the Ten Commandments or the fruits of the Spirit—and then showing how to apply these to their lives. Hopefully you built your own faith and shared it with them.

If you did, I would gladly congratulate you and then tell you there's more work to do.

If you did not, I would ask you to play catch-up as much as possible, using the principles of this chapter.

Let me preface my driver training comments by saying that I took primary responsibility for teaching all three of my children to drive. I did not send them to driving school, instead purchasing a parent-led course packet. As far as the hazardous duty of sitting next to my fledgling drivers, that was almost all me.

I experienced a mix of dad sighs and nail-biting, but I was typically very patient with them. During Anthony's first stint at more than thirty mph on a public street, I can recall suggesting that he might edge the car farther away from the curb and toward the center of the lane. As a passenger, I can't remember ever being that close to the curb!

We would always start the learning process by driving slowly around an empty school parking lot and parking in pull-in spaces. The most memorable moment was when Austin was headed into a parking space and briefly hit the gas instead of the brake. The problem was that there was a drop-off after the curb and a tree in front of the passenger! I hollered something akin to "Jesus, I'm coming to you!" before he could halt the car in time. (Austin claims I overstate the danger when I tell the story; I claim he didn't have the tree in front of him like I did.)

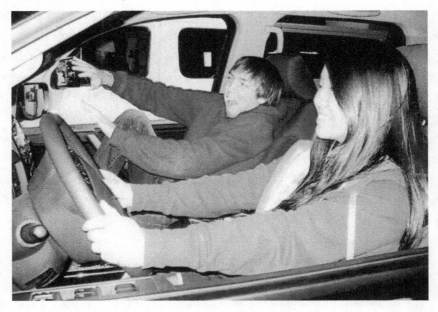

In Rebecca's case, I remember complaining a lot about her parking alignments and making her repeatedly try again. (Perhaps Austin was just as concerned in this photograph.)

Sara decided she did not want to participate in the training for various reasons. But at times, she wanted to give instructions from the back seat. Based on a traumatic episode when I was a teen driver, in which two parents and two grandparents all told me how to drive at the same time, Sara and I had agreed on a rule that there was only one guiding voice in the car. When Sara would begin backseat driving, I would say, "Do you want to sit up here? Because there's only one voice, and that comes from the passenger seat." Sara would say, "No." Sara would happily pipe down because she didn't truly want to be in the front passenger seat.

There's a unison parenting lesson here as we map from driver training to disciple training. My traumatic episode wasn't merely caused by too many voices but by too many opinions. When one backseat driver said, "Turn right," and another said, "Turn left," how could I function? Multiple voices weren't the problem as much as multiple messages.

> Multiple voices weren't the problem as much as multiple messages.

The same holds true for disciple training. I don't expect that every parenting partner will possess exactly the same beliefs. Partners may have grown up in different denominations or even different religions or no religion at all. But the messaging to the teen should be mutually agreed and then be consistent. I'll develop this thought momentarily.

The Decision to Train

The decision to train a student driver primarily depends on age, but it also considers the student's readiness and maturity. One of our children received their driver's license almost immediately after their sixteenth birthday, while another voluntarily waited more than a year before acquiring their license.

Once you've made the decision to train a driver, you must decide whether to outsource the training or take it on yourself. Even with outsourcing, there is typically a level of experience the teen must attain, such as fifty hours of driving, during which you would lead from the passenger seat. So, even with outsourcing, you carry a large responsibility.

The same goes for the decision to train a disciple. You may utilize a discipleship program at your church, but at the end of the day, you remain the primary discipler of your child.

This responsibility is largely based on the simple fact that you are around your child a lot more than anyone from the church is. Your daily interactions, your family values framework, your dinnertime discussions, your family meetings, and your own faith journey are all discipling influencers. You can also reinforce and model what the child is learning from any church class.

A critical unison parenting point is that all parenting partners must agree to the extra effort required for spiritual training. For example, in a divorce situation, the teen may move back and forth between houses. The spiritual training must remain consistent, such as the commitment to drive the child to church. It's possible that the divorced parents attend different churches, so decide on where the child will attend and how they will get there.

Preparing to Train

When the time came to train each driver, we parents (OK, mainly me) had to prepare. This meant checking on the new requirements (which changed between each child's training), selecting and purchasing a parent-led course, understanding what was required of the parent teacher, calculating the timelines and the fees, and so on.

Similarly, parents must prepare for disciple training. Some preparation is individual, while other preparation is done jointly by all parenting partners.

Nancy Montgomery suggests the following ideas as parenting partners prepare for disciple training.

1. **Clarify your own beliefs.** Take time to consider the questions: Do you believe in God? Do you believe there was a divine element in the creation of the world? What do you think happens when a person dies? If you and your parenting partner(s) have different beliefs, it's wise to decide what beliefs you will present in order to avoid confusing the child with different opinions.

2. **Consider what kind of spiritual education you want for your child.** Will your family join and participate in a church, synagogue, or other house of worship? Do you want your child to attend services regularly? Do you plan to send them to a private religious school or arrange other spiritual training? Many churches offer specialized training classes once the child reaches a certain age or maturity.

3. **If you don't believe in organized religion, instill kindly principles.** Encourage them to respect others' beliefs, learn right from wrong, develop a sense of family history, and demonstrate a caring attitude toward others.

4. **Build on family traditions.** Spirituality can connect us to the divine, to each other, and to the past. If you're raising your child in the same spiritual tradition that you were raised in, be sure they know that they are carrying on family rituals that were passed along by their grandparents and even great-grandparents.[62]

Let me append my thoughts regarding this list.

This preparation sequence is a time to consider how any opposing religious views will be presented. Earlier in the teen's development, it would be good to start with a single point of view, the main one you want to instill. Over time, healthy discussion of varying religious views could occur in the teen's presence or, better yet, driven by the teen's questions. Your child is learning critical thinking. The ability to compare and contrast views is important. Still, I recommend that, as unison parents, you return to the baseline view as the standard once different viewpoints are presented.

For example, there was a young man, "Adrian," who went to his parents and requested that he be allowed to attend his friend's church, apart from his family. In talking to the parents (and to my parenting classes), I recommended that the boy attend the other church perhaps once a month but continue to attend the family's church the rest of the time.

We're willing for you to experience other contexts, but your primary experience in our house will be in our preferred context.

The message is, "We are raising you in a certain context. We're willing for you to experience other contexts, but your primary experience in our house will be in our preferred context. As an adult, you can make your own decisions on where to attend."

Regarding family traditions, each origin family will certainly have different traditions, but some may overlap. For example, both Sara's and my families used an Advent calendar to anticipate the coming of Christmas. On the other hand, my family always attended Easter sunrise service, while Sara's family occasionally attended and put a lower priority on it.

As parenting partners prepare and bring out various traditions, it's good to unite on which ones will be carried forward, which ones will not, and what new traditions might be originated.

Handling the Big Questions

Your amoeba is entering a spiritual growth phase in which they begin pondering the big questions of life. Since parents will never know when those questions might come, you are wise to prepare some answers in advance. (However, it's also fine to research the answers together with your teen.)

If any religion is going to have validity, it has to have distinct answers to difficult questions of life, death, morality, and deity. In my view, it's important that Christianity indeed does offer solid answers to difficult questions. Those questions and answers are beyond the scope of this book; however, I can recommend a couple of books that delve into such questions from the perspective of traditional Christian tenets:

- *Mere Christianity*, C. S. Lewis (Harper Collins).
- *Restart: Getting Past Christian-ish*, Scott Engle (Crossbooks).

C. S. Lewis was a master of apologetics, the practice of answering objections to Christianity with logic; it's a fun exercise and is persuasive to some people. But we must remember that the best way to convince anyone, including your teen, of the value and truth of Christianity is by displaying faith turned into action.

No Social Passing

Let's talk about preparing for the intensity of driver and disciple training. When my eldest, Anthony, acquired his driver's license after taking a parent-sponsored course, he was not required to take that fearful driving test with an examiner in the car. But three years later, when it was Austin's turn, the parent-sponsored certificate did not exempt him from driving with the examiner. Why was this?

I'm pretty sure it was because of social passing.

You would think that a parent who not only cares for their child but retains tremendous financial liability for their child's driving would carefully teach the child to drive and drive well. That is surely the presumption on which the original law for parent-sponsored courses was built.

But my kids would tell me, "Dad, you're such a stickler for the rules and for the driving hours. Other parents just sign the form and let their kids go for the license."

Hence, the state had to modify the rules to ensure quality of driving from parent-sponsored students.

The parents were enacting what I call *social passing*. They put in no effort, required no effort, demanded no quality, and just checked the box so the parents didn't have to be bothered, and their kid could get a driver's license.

When it comes to spiritual training, don't socially pass your child.

When it comes to spiritual training, don't socially pass your child. Train them in the intended way.

How does this relate to your fledgling disciple? It means you must put in effort, require effort, and avoid simply checking boxes. I recall a parent-and-teen retreat when a high school mentor, "Caroline," shared her experience of disciple training and how her parents approached it.

- Generally speaking, the parents were only somewhat supportive of the church-led training and church in general.
- Caroline had to roust a parent out of bed each Sunday morning to even get driven to church.
- Worse, Caroline craved spiritual discussions with her parents, but because the parents weren't invested, that never happened. It deeply

wounded her that her parents did not participate in nor prioritize her spiritual training.

The experience pained Caroline so much that when it was her little brother's turn to go through the church training, she sat her parents down and said, "You're not going to do the same thing to him." Caroline revealed how distressed and lonely she felt. She challenged her parents to do better.

To their credit, they did. With the second opportunity, they became more supportive and got involved in church-sponsored parent activities like my parenting class.

When my children became adults, it was interesting to have adult conversations about my parenting. What clearly came out was that what I did was more impactful than what I said.

That's frightening! Events, conversations, decisions, and behaviors that I barely recall or don't recall had bigger impacts than I would have thought. Simply living my life as I did was an influential model for how my children would behave.

Simply living my life as I did was an influential model for how my children would behave.

For example, I recall Rebecca taking on a heavy course load and working two jobs in college. When I suggested that she trim back, Rebecca said, "Duh, I am following what I saw you do!"

This revelation really shouldn't surprise us. Danny Huerta, executive vice president of parenting and youth at Focus on the Family, says:

> *Our teaching and impact matters. Our children are wanting something. They're watching. They want to follow something, and that's why God made parents—because we get to be an extension of Him to our kids.*[63]

My message is: if you try to spiritually pass your child, if you simply tell them to go over there and develop themselves spiritually, and you don't model it yourself, and you don't get involved, then you are undermining the whole experience.

Just as you have to be in the car with them when they learn to drive, you must be in the "spiritual" car with them.

Just as you have to be in the car with them when they learn to drive, you must be in the "spiritual" car with them. Just as you can't toss them the keys and tell them to drive, you shouldn't ask them to undertake a spiritual formation process in which you are not involved.

Hesitations about Training

I would ask participants in my parenting classes, "What are your hesitations about teaching your child to drive?" Typical answers were:

- It's scary to ride with them!
- I'm not sure how to teach driving.
- I don't know all the rules by heart.
- I am not patient enough to teach them.
- I'm not a good enough driver myself.

Then I would ask, "What are your hesitations about being a discipling parent and teaching Christianity to your child?" The answers were similar:

- I'm scared.
- I'm not sure how to teach discipleship.
- I don't know the Bible by heart.
- I'm not patient enough to teach them.
- I'm not a good enough disciple myself.

From experience with fifteen years of parenting classes, I would say the biggest blocker is the parent's assessment of their knowledge of the Bible. But there's something we can do about that.

Engaging with Your Teen about the Bible

When it comes to driver training, do you have to know all the traffic rules by heart?

You know a lot of the laws from your own training and from experience, but if you just took the written test cold, you would probably score about an eighty-five. The reason for such a low score is that laws change, and recommendations of driving techniques have changed.

For example, the online driving material taught Rebecca that cars entering the freeway have right of way over the cars already on the freeway—opposite of what I learned and certainly not aligned with what I experience.

One of the richest parts of the parent-led driver training experience is the dialogue about what the teen driver is learning from books, classes, and videos. Usually it starts with them saying, "Dad/Mom, did you know that . . .?"

I suggest that the disciple training model would work similarly. Must you know the Bible by heart? You know parts of the Bible from your own training, study, and experience. If you took a Bible test cold, you would score . . . eighty-five? Maybe not!

Again, one of the richest parts of the parent-led disciple training experience could be the dialogue about what the teen is learning and what insight and experience you can offer on the topic. Again, the conversation might start with, "Dad/Mom, did you know that . . .?"

When Anthony was taking his church-led training, I learned that he decided to deep-dive into Revelation on his own. At that time, I had not read Revelation start to finish in a single, consistent pass. I felt like I should keep pace so we could have intelligent discussions about such a challenging, controversial part of the Bible, so I not only read Revelation start to finish, but I also found a study guide to help. We had some great discussions about the last book of the Bible.

Your child's spiritual growth is an opportunity to grow your own. If you want to teach them to be a disciple, follow Alicia von Stamitz's suggestion and:

Secure your own oxygen mask. The word "spiritual" derives from the Latin spiritus, meaning "wind" or "breath." If you want your child to breathe in deeply the spirit of God, you too must breathe deeply.[64]

Don't be intimidated by your child's growing knowledge of the Bible. Face it, your child is entering a stage of life when they are quite capable of teaching *you* a number of topics. Be vulnerable, be open to the experience, and share the adventure with them.

Outside the Book

In driver training, you'll encounter topics taught outside the book. The teen driver needs more than rules to operate a motor vehicle. They need additional experience of two kinds.

First, there are things to know about cars: changing a tire, safety features of the car, parts of the car, and what to do in an emergency.

My young drivers had to learn how to deal with mishaps. Anthony did a great job of steering the car and our family to safety when he suffered a blow-out on a country highway. Later, Austin experienced a blown engine while driving alone during rush hour on one of the busiest highways in our metropolitan area. Smoke began filling up the passenger cabin. A helpful driver pulled alongside and shouted, "You have smoke coming out the back!" Choking on the cabin smoke, Austin thanked him. No kidding, there's smoke out the back! Inside too!

Second, your teen driver needs practical driving experience. In the parent-led course, the teen needed to drive fifty hours. I loved a rule that was instituted by the time Rebecca was learning: the teen also had to watch *you* drive for ten hours.

I found this was a great way to teach her practical driving experience. I could talk about what I was seeing, what I was dealing with, the choices I was making, and why I made certain moves. In other words, I could teach her about driving situations based on my experience.

How do these two factors that went beyond "the book"—knowing about cars and practical driving experience—map to disciple training?

As Christians, we go beyond the book—the Bible—when we apply its messages to our seven-day practical faith journey. We must apply them to daily activities. We must apply them to big events, such as crises or landmark decisions.

Just as a parent can talk about their driving decisions to their teen, a parent can also talk about their choices as a disciple when talking to a teen.

- You might discuss choices from the past or the present or even choices you're contemplating for the future.
- You can talk about how you maintain your faith, how you deal with temptation, and how you deal with people who don't treat you well.
- You can turn these discussions around to ask them questions, such as how they will maintain their faith, how they will deal with temptation, and so forth.

We started this section talking about why you might be hesitant to lead your child's discipleship training. I hope you can see that you each have a lot to offer in sharing and teaching each other. In addition, your parenting partners can have the same kinds of discipling discussions, each in their own way, but with the same intent of creating dialogue and a spiritual foundation for the teen.

Let's talk further about how practical driving experience maps to practical disciple experience.

Are They Ready?

A new father asked me when one of my kids started driving, "When they can drive on their own, do things get easier or harder?"

My response was, "Yes."

It gets easier because your schedule changes, and you don't have to drive them everywhere. It gets harder because you worry more and expend more energy in supporting their driving.

But the number one question people asked me when I turned my kids loose with the car keys and a fresh license was, *Are they ready?*

My response was, "I don't know."

I mean, my kids were well-prepared. They had knowledge, plenty of practice, and disciplined traits. But what would they do in a moment of distraction or crisis or split-second decision-making? I didn't know what they would do in critical moments. There is no way to easily simulate such occasions.

The child that I least expected to have a driving issue wound up totaling a car, escaping serious injury in the process, and piling up speeding tickets. So you never know.

I think the best you can do is to prepare them for situations. Review situations that can come up and dissect how to react to them.

Similarly, our youth are driving in heavy spiritual traffic each day, where there is impurity and temptation. Similarly, we should review with them situations that can come up and how to react to them.

In both cases, you have to deal with mistakes and bad decisions.

- Driving: getting lost, driving carelessly, having an accident.
- Discipling: getting lost in a different way, being careless in a different way, having accidents in a different way.

Both driving and discipling are about making choices, staying focused, and putting education and good intentions into practice.

Both are about making choices, staying focused, and putting education and good intentions into practice.

Planning for Situations

One of my mottos for parenting is to teach your children how to plan for situations. This can be considered part of the decision-making model shown earlier in the book, but we must ratchet it up another level in the teen years.

In driving, we talked to our teens about weather conditions, what happens if you're too tired to drive home, driving into unfamiliar areas, etc.

In discipling, we talked to our teens about bad party situations and how to remove yourself from them, how to deal with people who challenge Christian faith, and how to be a light in the world without getting caught up in worldly things.

For example, we talked about using parents as an excuse to get out of any situation you didn't want to be in. Our kids didn't have to explain why they wanted to elude the situation. The parents were the scapegoats to allow them to save face and to have a sure way to depart. Parenting partners need to be in sync on whether and how to adopt this technique.

The parents were the scapegoats to allow teens to save face and to have a sure way of getting free.

Each child had a code word or phrase to alert us to their desire to come home. For Anthony, it was *headache*. He might call or text us to say he had a headache. Our job was to recognize and respond—actually, to overreact. "You know how you get when you feel a headache coming on. This might be a migraine again. You can't afford to lose a couple of days. You must come home immediately."

Those statements were mostly but not completely true, yet they were useful to allow him to pin the blame on us so he could escape.

For Rebecca, the code word was *permission*. She would say, "Do I have your permission to do such-and-such?"—for instance, stay at the party longer or go to someone else's house. When we heard the word *permission*, we were supposed to give the answer, "No, you **don't** have our permission. You need to come home right away. The evening is over."

She still gives me a rough time because on the first occasion to use this system, I forgot! She asked for permission, and I said, "Sure! Go ahead!" Rebecca was forced to say, "Dad, I don't think you heard me well. Do I have your PERMISSION to go to boba tea?" Then I fumbled around, "Oh! Oh, no! You don't have permission. You must come home right away." A father retraining session occurred when she arrived home.

Austin's word? *falafel.* As in, "I'm craving some falafel, Dad. Can we get some?" I never understood that one, and fortunately, we never had to use it!

I will tell you that I have had a number of families from my parenting classes come back to me and say how useful the system was. One mother told me that she honestly didn't see how the system was necessary until her three teenagers were grateful to use it to dodge delicate situations.

Be a Light

I mentioned above how we would talk to our children about how to be a light in the world without getting caught up in worldly things.

We placed our kids in public schools; the schools are excellent in our city. But I questioned myself one time when a home-schooling parent indirectly criticized our decision and expressed the advantages of sheltering kids from temptations and evil.

Questioning myself and how we might have exposed our children, I went to our high school senior, Anthony, and asked, "What would you say that Mom and I taught you about attending public school as a Christian?"

Anthony said, "You taught me to be a light in the world, to not be influenced negatively by others, and to influence them positively instead."

I could not have phrased it any better. That is exactly the message I wanted him to soak in.

Taken altogether, we had prepared our children for situations they would face, part of the disciple training I've been talking about.

Transferring Ownership

It's hard to hand the car keys over to a teenager. As the parent of adult children, I can tell you it's also tough, but equally exciting, to watch your grown kids purchase their own cars and use their freedom to drive wherever they will.

The purpose of disciple training is to eventually hand the keys of their faith over to them. When they were children, we protected and nurtured their faith. But as they grow, their faith becomes theirs and theirs alone. It is unlikely to exactly mirror our own. That too is hard to watch and hard to swallow. But it's exciting in its own way.

188 | Unison Parenting

> God doesn't have grandchildren. All individuals are direct
> children of God. Our children don't inherit our faith.

A phrase I have heard several times is true: God doesn't have grandchildren. All individuals are direct children of God. Our children don't inherit our faith. We don't stand between them and God. Ultimately, each person stands alone before God; hence, it's right that they own their beliefs and spirituality and are responsible.

I understand how conflicting your emotions can be. You may be as frightened for their souls as you are for their physical bodies behind the wheel. But our job as parents is to provide a sound spiritual foundation. The rest is up to them and to the Holy Spirit. You see, the Holy Spirit is the ultimate discipler. The Spirit will always be nearby and will always be working to bring your child closer to their heavenly Father. Pray to the Spirit and trust the Spirit to tend to your child's soul; pray for your child to be receptive and accepting in return.

An Impassioned Plea from Me to You

I was a church youth group counselor for thirty-plus years. No kidding, I saw it all. I won't list "it all" here. But I did see the best a youth group or a youth or an adult can be, and I saw the worst that a youth group or a youth or an adult could be.

I saw the kids and families that bought in and the kids and families that didn't. And I saw their long-term results as well.

So one of my strongest, most confident recommendations in this book is for you to push for and commit to your teen participating fully in your church's youth program.

> Push for and commit to your teen participating fully in
> your church's youth program.

To emphasize, this does not mean you are outsourcing your child's spiritual formation. You're still the primary discipler. But you're enlisting a powerful partner to provide benefits that you cannot.

Let me share these six primary reasons for your teen to become an active member of that youth program.

1. They will be influenced by positive Christian people.

Peers are very important to teens. A church youth group is a place where they can experience Christian peers that model proper behavior and spiritual formation.

Look, I'm not going to affirm that every youth group attendee is great. I knew of teens that put on a show of doing the right thing, then switched to treating others poorly when the adults left the room.

But as a whole, strong Christian youth are extremely influential on other teens. They become a vital part of your child's spiritual growth.

So do caring adults. Again, I could say the same thing to a teen that a parent did, and it carried a different weight. It's been a huge blessing of my life to have teens grow into adults, see me years later, and tell me what an influence I had on their lives. Your child can experience the same relationship and mentoring from a caring, trustworthy adult.[e]

2. They will experience a safe place to be themselves.

I can't stress this enough: Your child has the capability to take on a different persona at church than they do at school. This allows them to get away from

---

e   More and more churches are creating safe environments through adult training and guidelines to protect young people in light of past abuses. We'll never see perfection, but when followed, such training and guidelines do protect everyone, including the adults.

whatever way they're trying to fit in at school and simply act as their real selves, knowing they are accepted.

I've seen this work for kids who go to a church where not many from their school attend. They find that they can be totally open about what's going on at school, receiving support, advice, and love in the process.

I've also seen this work for kids who go to school with each other. Students who are being bullied have found support when they return to school, as they have explained to youth group peers what it feels like to be bullied. Or a youth might make friends in the church environment that they never would in the school environment.

3. They will engage in wholesome, safe activities.

If you're looking for wholesome, safe activities for your child, what better place than church? I've marveled at parents who cry out that there's no place where their kids can experience such activities. Uh, the church?

Not only that, but your teen can also experience adventures that are not easily found elsewhere. Sponsored camps, retreats, mission trips, and other outings expose your child to a wider world and to people who are not like themselves.

Having said that, let me emphasize that the big events on their own do not create a firm foundation. There is nothing more vital to spiritual formation than the regular, repeated, weekly visits to a youth program.

4. They will hear faith expressed in their language.

Your teenager might not seem responsive to the worship style that you prefer.

But get them in a contemporary worship setting with their peers, and they might engage in passionate worship.

In youth group, the Word is passed along in ways and with examples designed expressly for teens. The media used is teen-friendly. They can express their faith in teen language too.

5. They will have participation and leadership opportunities.

What growth opportunities are offered within youth groups! Your child might become a small group leader. They might join the youth worship band. They might find a service suborganization in which they can participate or lead.

I feel like it's become harder and harder in many schools for a child to experience leadership opportunities, especially as school populations grow and programs are cut. Usually there are plenty of existing opportunities for leadership in a church, and more can be created by insightful adult leaders.

6. They will receive a spiritual foundation for life.

Believe this: many teenagers are able to use the spiritual springboard of youth group to become faithful adults.

Now, I'm not going to kid you. Everyone knows that the college years are a time when it is easy for even the most faithful youth to fall away. But with a foundation, they have a better chance to stay connected to God and to the church as they mature.

Overcoming the Main Objection

The number one reason that a teen will tell you they don't want to attend youth group this week is "I don't know anybody" or "My friend won't be there, and I don't know anyone else."

Your answer? "Just go!"

Why? "Because you will make new friends. Maybe not tonight, but over time."

I can **promise** you that this works. Let me give you three notable examples of a phenomenon I saw repeated many times.

When Anthony entered sixth grade, I was excited for him to join me in the youth program as my first child to do so. However, he felt like he had no friends. By September, he didn't want to go to Sunday school or to Sunday evening youth meetings. But I encouraged him to keep going to see what would happen. Grudgingly, he did.

In November, he found me after Sunday school and said, "Stephen H. came and sat down next to me today. And Steven P. came over and sat with me too! I can't believe it!"

I said, "Do you know why they came and sat with you?"

"No," he replied.

I then explained to him how neither Stephen H. nor Steven P. were consistent at going to youth activities. "When they walked in the room, they felt like they didn't know anyone, so they looked for a familiar face. Because you are always there, you're a familiar face to the kids who are inconsistent, and they will gravitate to you. So the key is to go every week, and you'll have people look to you to be their friend."

Before Christmas arrived, Anthony had a group of five or so friends that hung out together, all centered around the fact that he was the consistent one.

Years later, a lady approached me about her nephew, "Nathan." She explained that Nathan was entering eighth grade and considering entering our membership training program for youth, but her brother and his wife were not receptive (mainly because they didn't want to be bothered with driving him). Nathan was shy and disconnected, so his primary hesitation was that he didn't know anyone.

The aunt wanted me to talk to the family about the reasons for going. We arranged a hallway meeting that day between services.

I explained the different features of the youth program, the particular training, and the opportunities for participation. I assured the family as an adult leader that I would keep an eye on Nathan and ensure he was making friends. Then I told Anthony's story of the benefits of consistent participation.

Nathan decided to join; I could tell his parents weren't happy.

True to my word, I introduced Nathan to other kids. I would arrange it so he never sat alone. (By the way, we counselors were always making sure no one sat alone.) Nathan experienced a good introduction to the youth program during the year-long training.

Afterward, Nathan kept going with the youth group. He found his niche in youth choir and became very dedicated to it. Nathan emerged as one of the important members of the choir as his voice matured.

My final example is a little different. It's the story of two girls, "Lauren" and "Holly," who went to different middle schools. Both were little sisters of youth group members and were having a difficult time early on finding friends. But they eventually connected with each other and struck up a marvelous friendship. They even became college roommates. It's a wonderful story of friendship found at church.

Keep pushing; keep encouraging. Your child **will** find friends!

A church youth group is a great place for wholesome, safe activities. But our teenagers are surrounded by temptation and impurity. How can you try to prevent them from experiencing the consequences of an impure world? That's the subject of the next chapter.

Summary of Formative Parenting

Key Points

- Driver training is similar to disciple training. In both cases, you retain primary responsibility, even if others help.
- Parenting partners often don't want to expend the effort on spiritual training. This can be painful for a child who wants to share the experience and partner as they grow spiritually.
- Address your hesitations about disciple training, especially regarding your Bible knowledge. Learn the Bible together with your teen as necessary.
- The Holy Spirit is the ultimate discipler of your child. You still have a role: to provide the environment for a spiritual foundation.
- Get your teen into a church youth group!

Unison Parenting Foundation

- Parenting partners must consider disciple training and all agree to execute it. This requires a coordinated commitment and extra effort.
- Once decided, you must align on the approach after clarifying your own beliefs, considering specialized alternatives, and unifying on the primary religious messages to communicate to your child.
- Help your teen plan for critical life situations. Get organized on how the parents can help the teen escape uncomfortable situations.

Preventative Parenting

Meditation: Ephesians 6:1–3

"Children, obey your parents in the Lord, for this is right. 'Honor your father and mother'—which is the first commandment with a promise—'so that it may go well with you and that you may enjoy long life on the earth.'"

Teens don't have to rebel to ignore their parents.

It's human nature to ignore advice. Think of us reading this book: Even now, do we do everything our parents say? Did you as a child?

Even if advice is good, we may ignore it. Yet taking advice, or at least deeply considering it, is a way that we honor whoever lends the advice.

The verse we have today—directly from Ephesians and indirectly from Exodus 20—is something we should teach our children from the beginning, as part of our family framework. It doesn't mean the parents are always right or that they never have to apologize. It does mean that their guidance and lived experiences and roles in children's lives should be honored.

In this chapter on preventative parenting, parents are urged to give, and teens are urged to receive, advice that is based on the lived experience of many. You parents are urged to adopt these ideas as family policy. Teens are urged to follow their parents' lead, both honoring and trusting their parents in the process.

The expected result? That things will go well with our young people during a phase when their very lives may be at stake if they ignore the advice.

The Genesis of This Lesson

As I've mentioned, I taught parenting classes to parents of teens in my home church for fifteen years. One of the most popular lessons was this one on preventative parenting.

What I'm about to tell you has been taught to more than seven hundred families. There have been a lot of positive responses and a lot of dialogue about this lesson and its implementation, probably more so than any lesson I've prepared. This lesson has had a huge positive impact on families, and I pray that it will do the same for yours.

The genesis of this lesson came about in the same year that I was starting to teach parenting classes. It began with a startling moment that became a victory moment in our family.

"Just Like You Said It Would"

One day, when Anthony was in seventh grade, he entered the house after walking home from school and announced, "Dad! It finally happened! I got offered drugs today!"

Seeing the startled look on my and Sara's faces, he added, "And I turned them down!"

Whew!

Then Anthony said, "And Dad, it happened just the way you told me it would happen."

I say a lot of things and then forget them. So I needed him to play it back. "What did I tell you, son?"

Anthony answered, "You told me two things I didn't believe: that someone would offer me drugs in middle school, and that it would be a friend that offered me and not some guy on the street corner."

Then I remembered both those pieces of advice. From my youth ministry experience, I had told my kids that drugs were not just abused in high school but that middle schoolers had the same issues, so to be wary about being offered drugs in middle school.

I had also told them that the offer wouldn't come from some guy on the sidewalk with a trench coat, opening it and saying, "Hey kid, do you want some drugs?" Instead, the offer would come from a friend who would make it sound like something completely normal.

The offer of drugs won't come from a guy in a trench coat on the street corner. It'll come from a friend who will make it sound normal.

Anthony described what happened. A classmate (not truly a friend) was walking with him as they left school. As they neared his house, he asked Anthony, "Would you like to come into my house and smoke some pot? My parents aren't home."

Anthony was startled but regained his footing, using a technique I've mentioned before to throw parents under the bus. "No, I have to get home. My parents are expecting me home on time so I can do some chores for them."

We praised him and were thankful for how he beautifully handled the situation, so thankful that on Sunday at my adult Sunday school class, I raised a concern and a joy that Anthony had been offered drugs but had turned them down, in the manner that he had been instructed.

My fellow parents asked, "What did you tell him?" The class was running late, so I said, "It's a bit of a long story." They responded, "Would you please teach us a class next week on what you and Sara did to prepare him?" And I agreed.

In preparing the lesson, I was sure my story wouldn't fill forty-five minutes, so I did some research on antidrug techniques. I came across a terrific website based on the US government's "Parents—The Anti-Drug" ad campaign running at that time. (Please see the ninth tip below for more current resources that you can research.)

In reading the eleven tips on the site, I realized these were all things that Sara and I had already been doing or were preparing to do as our kids got older. So I based the lesson on these principles. Over time, I added more stories of parents and children to flesh out the principles. What follows is the culmination of iterating this lesson over fifteen years.

Eleven Tips for Preventative Parenting

As you read through these, you'll notice that these are not eleven tips for stopping drug use per se. They are eleven sound principles intended to prevent a variety of bad things happening to your teen. In other words, the tips represent good parenting.

There are references to the drugs of focus at the time and to scenarios from that era. While most are still relevant, I will address in my comments more recent substance abuse developments, such as opioids, and recent views on mental health and depression.

I will list the original text from the government site (which no longer exists, though other similar sites have replaced it) and add my comments.

1. Set Rules

Let your teen know that drug and alcohol use is unacceptable and that these rules are set to keep him or her safe. Set limits with clear consequences for breaking them.

I advise clearly telling your teen, "I expect that you will not use alcohol until you are legal drinking age. Period."

When told this, every one of my kids said, "I know that, Dad."

My response was, "I want to make sure there is no confusion about what I believe and expect. I don't know what you will do, but you cannot think that you don't know where I stand."

As discussed in an earlier chapter, parties where alcohol is being served are best avoided.

2. Praise and Reward

Praise and reward good behavior for compliance and enforce consequences for non-compliance.

This is Parenting 101, and we've covered it already in this book.

I would add that despite expecting good behavior, it doesn't hurt to praise your teen for making good choices, especially regarding the items on this list. Also remember the frustration of Ronald, whose strict parents never loosened the reins to reward his good choices. Positive behavior should eventually be rewarded with more options, later curfews, etc.

3. Know Where Your Teen Is

Know where your teen is and what he or she will be doing during unsupervised time. Research shows that teens with unsupervised time are three times more likely to use marijuana or other drugs. Unsupervised teens are also more likely to engage in risky behaviors such as underage drinking, sexual activity, and cigarette smoking than other teens. This is particularly important after school, in the evening hours, and also when school is out during the summer or holidays.

All activities should have clear start and stop times. You should also be aware, through your teen's communication, of where they are at all times.

When I was a teen, my parents had this rule. If I was at Jimmy's house and wanted to go to David's house, I had to call them and get their approval. Sara and I applied this rule as well. It generally went well; we did have a few issues with it at times, mostly differing over whether the next destination was a good idea.

One of my favorite sayings that parents have played back to me as something they used effectively was, "No one in this family has a blank check." A mother recently wrote me to say, *"We used a lot of your teaching in discussion with our children and said many times, 'You do not have a blank check to do whatever you want!'"*

No one in this family has a blank check to do whatever they want.

Perhaps the blank check analogy will require some explanation or an update for today's teens who don't know what a check is! Perhaps a blank permission slip. The idea is that the teen does not get to fill in the blanks of when, where, what, how, etc. This is done in consultation with the parent. Start and stop times are clearly defined, along with the approved activities.

I mentioned earlier my many questions to my teens when they brought in their requests and how I would send them out for more research. There was a variation I developed through practical application, as sometimes the teen group they were joining did not have a view of the whole evening, so some details were hazy.

The way I addressed this was to set up a midpoint of the evening where the child would check in to give a status update and to say what the group was planning to do next. It's an option to offer as they build trust with you, and it works very well. My daughter and I did this a lot. She would call at 9:00 to say, "We finished the movie," and then reveal the next proposed steps. Sometimes she didn't want to participate and would use her code word with me. Other times, the entire group had worn out and planned to return to their homes.

I recommend the midpoint as a way to confirm plans and establish a final curfew. For example, if you know they're selecting a 9:10 movie that will run two hours at a theater fifteen minutes away, perhaps you can relax that 11:30 curfew a bit to adapt to previews, brief goodbyes, etc. Share your thinking with them, such as "The movie should let out around 11:25, so I expect you home by 11:45." This allows you to maintain oversight while offering reasonable flexibility, which your teen will appreciate.

4. Talk to Your Teens

While shopping or riding in the car, casually ask them how things are going at school, about their friends, what their plans are for the weekend, etc.

OK, here is the **GOLD** I promised in the book's introduction!

I got this advice from a parenting role model of mine whose eldest daughter was several years older than my eldest. He told me if you want to get your kids to talk to you, do this; it's so good, I directly highlighted it in the box below.

Talk to your teen after 11 p.m. in their room.

Instead of trying to wrangle information out of them at the dinner table (which is still an important meeting place daily, if possible, for family time), go to their room for a one-on-one talk after 11 p.m.

Does this work? Let me cite these examples:

- It absolutely worked with every one of my children.
- Giving this advice to the seven hundred families, I have never had anyone coming back to say that it didn't work; if it didn't, I don't know about it. Instead, I've had many parents praise this technique as working—and all too well.
- In fact, parents complain about the technique because they themselves are tired at 11 p.m. Here is a typical comment I would hear:

"I was so tired, but my child kept talking, and I didn't want to miss any-thing! But it was hard to hold up my end. I could barely keep my eyes open!"

Why does it work? One reason is obvious; the other is subtle.

1. It's a well-known fact that teens are more active and alert late at night, while they are neither active nor alert early in the morning. This is why some schools have shifted their high school hours later. You're catching them at a peak hour.

2. When you go to their room, you are on their turf, not yours. They are more comfortable in their room than out in the dining room or living room. Also, you're likely to catch them at a time when they're happy and relaxed with their music or whatever is going on at 11 p.m.

I don't think you can underrate the idea of adapting to them rather than them having to adapt to you. By adapting to the way they function, you're going to get great results and become closer to your teen.

5. Keep Them Busy

Keep them busy—especially between 3 p.m. and 6 p.m. and into the evening hours. Engage your teen in after-school activities. Enroll your child in a supervised educational program or a sports league. Research shows that teens who are involved in constructive, adult-supervised activities are less likely to use drugs than other teens.

I agree with keeping your children busy and active; it's a very positive approach, but . . .

We can also overschedule our children and drive them crazy. This is a key unison parenting point, to be on the same page regarding children's schedules. Sara and I tried to prevent overscheduling with guardrails such as, "You can only  play one sport at a time." Baseball in the spring and football in the fall was fine, but trying to play fall baseball along with football was disallowed.

There is a tradeoff between busy-ness and anxiety. A youth pastor once said to parents, "If we expect kids to act like adults, we will force adult problems on them, and they will find adult solutions." Such as alcohol and drugs, which you were trying to prevent them from using in the first place.

> If we expect kids to act like adults, we will force adult problems on them, and they will find adult solutions.

I want to add a comment about the 3–6 p.m. window, which is between school and dinner. A lot of kids follow latchkey lives and are unsupervised during this time. Not surprisingly, I once saw a statistic that late at night is <u>not</u> the peak of sexual activity among teens; instead, it is between 3 and 6 p.m.

My son Anthony witnessed how this bore out while working at a famous fast food chicken restaurant noted for family values. The workers looked out the window at 5 p.m. at a parked car in their lot moving and shaking. They called the police, who came to fetch two teens having sex in the car. Unbelievable, right?

6. Check on Your Teenager
Occasionally check in to see that your kids are where they say they're going to be and that they are spending time with whom they say they are with.

This echoes number three above. In the **Attentive Parenting** chapter, I'll talk more about techniques used to check on your teenager.

I'd like to insert a real-life story of checking on your teenager in your own home. This is the narrative of seventh-grader "Drew" and his tenth-grade sister, "Rose," two teens I knew personally through my church's youth group.

Drew and his friend wanted to try cigarettes. They enjoyed the buzz so much, they wondered what else was out there.

Over a blindingly fast six weeks, Drew and his friend accelerated through alcohol, marijuana, and harder drugs. Rose was also using such substances and enabled Drew's experimentation. Rose showed Drew how to sneak out at night and not get caught; their house's layout was that the parents' bedroom was at one end, and the children's rooms at the other end. The parents had no idea of their children's nightly, rambling whereabouts.

It wasn't unusual for Drew to sneak out after midnight and arrive back home before daybreak. Between his exhaustion due to lack of sleep and his substance use, Drew's academic performance nose-dived.

The run came to an end after Drew was caught distributing cocaine at his middle school. Only one thing saved him: unbeknownst to Drew, he was actually selling fake cocaine. Because of that, he was not arrested, but he was expelled and sent to rehab with several of his new, drug-using friends.

Six weeks—that's all the time it took for Drew to go from smoking his first cigarette to rehab.

Six weeks—that's all the time it took for Drew to go from smoking his first cigarette to rehab.

It sounds like an impossible story. A good question is how Rose and Drew's parents did not realize something was going on with their children. I have never heard their explanation; I'm guessing it's not a very good one.

I have several more stories of drug-related behavior from thirty years of youth ministry, but I'll share just one more. While attending a different church and working with the youth during a Sunday night free-form time, I noticed how lethargic "Pete" and "Max" were acting compared to normal. Students were not supposed to leave the building, but through the kitchen window, I saw Pete and Max digging through the glove compartment of Pete's car.

When they returned, I scolded them for leaving. Soon after, I noticed a huge change in their behaviors. Pete and Max had both gone from being lethargic to giddy. They were boisterous and funny, cracking up several of the youth with their loud jokes and odd behavior. Then they seemed to wind down again.

I had recently taken drug training. To me, their behavior was a sign of possible cocaine use.

Privately, I approached their parents separately to describe their behavior and my concern. Both sets of parents laughed me off, saying their kids would never use drugs.

I don't have a firm recollection of what followed. I always have wondered whether I was right, and their parents addressed the possibility. Probably not.

So, yes, check on your teenager in multiple ways. Monitor them for signs of negative change in school performance, home behavior, and interest in friends and cherished activities.

7. Establish a Core Values Statement for Your Family

Consider developing a family mission statement that reflects your family's core values. This might be discussed and created during a family meeting or over a weekend meal together. Talking about what they stand for is particularly important at a time when teens are pressured daily by external influencers on issues like drugs, sex, violence, or vandalism. If there is no compass to guide your kids, the void will be filled by the strongest force.

In my view, techniques like the Choices Chart help establish the framework for not only parents but for children. They can understand what the core values are. Still, you may want to go beyond the Choices Chart.

A family mission statement may sound daunting. I'll tell you a great place to find core values: church! Between your church's understanding of mission and themes espoused by the children's program and youth group, you have a lot of sources to help you define your family mission statement.

8. Spend Time Together

Spend time together as a family regularly and be involved in your kid's lives. Create a bond with your child. This builds up credit with your child so that when you have to set limits or enforce consequences, it's less stressful.

When young parents ask me for advice (or even when they don't), I give them the line I shared earlier about fully experiencing every age with your children. That way, you have no regrets when they're grown because you didn't miss anything.

Otherwise, this advice of spending time together comes from "Introduction to People Management." It's an essential part of families, organizations, businesses, churches, and personal relationships.

Families should make new memories together.

One guiding thought I've found is to make new memories together. (This works well with old friends too.) It's not enough to talk about the old days, especially as they get into high school. Strive to have family outings, activities, or trips, and try new things, letting yourself be guided by each child's interests as a family and in one-on-one settings.

9. Take Time to Learn the Facts

Learn the facts about marijuana and underage drinking and talk to your teen about its harmful health, social, learning, and mental effects on young users.

AND . . . take time to learn the facts of sharing or distributing pornographic selfies on the internet (an illegal activity, even for teens, even for those who receive and reshare the photos).

AND . . . cutting.

AND . . . what today's pop songs are really saying.

AND . . . what their slang and emojis mean.

AND . . . how social media affects teen brains mentally and emotionally.

An educated parent can more easily interpret what's going on with their child and their child's friends when armed with this kind of information.

I have a funny example from youth ministry. In the decade of the 2010s, I was leading a covenant group of young men who met weekly. About the time they were fourteen or fifteen, a popular song came out called "Turn Down for What?" I had no idea what it meant, but it looked like teen slang, so I researched it.

At our next group meeting, the guys were playing the song, and I piped up, "Do you know what that song means?"

They didn't. I continued, "*Turn up* means to get high. *Turn down* means to get sober. The singer is saying, 'Give me a reason to get sober. I don't understand why I have to.' "

I never heard those boys play or refer to that song again.

In the decade of the 2000s, the antidrug campaign focused on marijuana's role as a gateway to harder drugs. Hence the focus in tip nine regarding marijuana.

Today, marijuana laws are becoming more relaxed, and the medicinal aspect is becoming better understood and leveraged. Still, much like alcohol, as marijuana is gradually legalized, it will certainly be authorized for legal adult use only.

Opioid abuse, especially with fentanyl, is what has been ramping up in recent years. Deaths from fentanyl are skyrocketing as dosages within seemingly innocuous street pills can kill. Incredibly potent and easy to get, the synthetic opioid has overtaken heroin as the drug most frequently involved in overdose deaths in the United States. It is linked to more fatalities of Americans under fifty than any other cause of death, including heart disease, cancer, and suicide.[65]

Parents need to understand the dangers their child faces from alcohol and drugs. Please refer to the **Useful Links and QR Codes** section for current information on substance use and abuse.

10. Get to Know Your Teen's Friends

Get to know your teen's friends (and their parents) by inviting them over for dinner or talking with them at your teen's soccer practice, dance rehearsal, or other activities.

A huge piece of advice is to host the teen gathering place. You will be able to track your teenager's activities while also meeting their friends. Be that household with food, games, and a willingness for late nights and unexpected arrivals.

Just as important is getting to know the parents of your teen's friends. This is more difficult. A great time to start this is before your child begins driving, when you are picking them up and dropping them off. Use those occasions to not just be a shuttle service but to walk to the door and talk with parents.

I'll have more to say on this topic in the following chapter, **Attentive Parenting**.

11. Stay in Touch with Adult Supervisor

These may be camp counselors, coaches, employers, or teachers. Have them inform you of any changes in your teen. Warning signs of drug use

include distance from family and existing friends, hanging out with a new circle of friends, lack of interest in personal appearance, or changes in eating or sleeping habits.

I can't stress enough how important it is to have trustworthy, caring adults in your child's life. Each of my children had such leaders in our church, as well as in other activities; I was so grateful for them. Influential schoolteachers were also instrumental.

Your children need adult role models. They already have role models in you, but they need others, even if you are a role model for other families' teens. Try to place your kids in activities and situations where positive, safe adults can interact with them.

Sometimes those adult supervisors may have more insight into what's going on with your teen than you do. For example, there were many times that a parent wanted to know from me, "Is my kid normal?" Because I saw a wide range of youth, I could give them perspective. A parent would ask whether a certain aspect of their child's behavior was normal; I wish I had a dollar for every time I told a parent, "Yes, it's normal."

But I could also tell when something wasn't normal. That was the case when I approached a father to let him know that I felt his son was exhibiting signs of depression; after I talked to the young man further, the son *admitted* he was feeling depressed and suicidal.

Thanks to the father's response to that conversation, he was able to intervene and stabilize the situation with his son.

Mental health and depression get much more attention these days than two decades ago, and it's a good thing.

Mental health and depression get much more attention these days than two decades ago, and it's a good thing. The stigma of mental illness is beginning to go away as people see what a huge problem it is, with 1 in 6 Americans estimated to have depression.

Especially encouraging is the attitude of your teen's generation. There is much more open discussion these days. Unfortunately, it's partially because of the unique stressors that members of Gen Z (born between 1997 and 2012) are facing.

Just 45 percent of Gen Z members report that their mental health is very good or excellent, according to the American Psychological Association. All other generation groups fared better on this statistic, including millennials (56 percent), Gen X members (51 percent), and boomers (70 percent).[66]

A 2022 Walton Family Foundation survey indicated 82 percent of Gen Z members label mass school shootings as something that needs to stop "right now," the highest issue in the poll. General mass shootings and gun violence were tied for second at 72 percent.[67] Other Gen Z stressors these days include political turmoil, climate change, student debt, job concerns, and leftover pandemic stress.

Not every Gen Z subgroup, of course, reacts the same to these stressors.

- While females are more likely to contemplate and plan suicide, males represented 80 percent of suicides in 2020 for ages fifteen to twenty-four.
- Gen Z members of color are more likely to commit suicide than whites.
- Suicide attempts for homosexual or bisexual students are about four times higher than for heterosexual students.
- In communities of color, mental health issues are more stigmatized than in white communities.[68]

While social media has clearly increased pressure and expectations on young people, leading to depression and other psychological problems, social media has helped to normalize mental health through interconnectedness and shared understanding.[69]

As with alcohol and drugs, it is best to get educated on how to identify and deal with depression. Please refer to the **Useful Links and QR Codes** section for a Mayo Clinic link regarding depression.

And, of course, ask adult supervisors their opinion if you have questions. Hopefully, they will honestly and carefully identify your teen's situation as normal or abnormal.

To wrap up this section, I have a stump to stand on regarding positive male role models from the ages of thirteen to fifteen.

My observation from thirty-plus years of youth ministry is that thirteen to fifteen is a very vulnerable, uncertain time for your teen girl. Weird things are happening to her body. Most girls do not feel good about themselves, especially the physical aspect.

As a result, girls thirteen to fifteen tend to look to an adult male role model to validate them. Believe me when I say this: If they do not find that adult male role model at home, they will find him somewhere. And you may not like who they find!

I could walk around the youth area on Sunday nights and be able to identify the girls in that age range who had good relationships with their fathers and those who did not. It's hard to explain—more of a feel from being around kids—but let's say I could sense more security and confidence with such girls.

I remember a girl, "Ashlee," in that age range who was new to the youth group. I quickly befriended her, and we got along well. But a month after she joined, I was walking past her talking to a group of girls, and she said, "Cecil is my best friend."

What? There is something really wrong there, I thought.

Fortunately, Ashlee had found a "best friend" with some character who did not take advantage of that situation. Instead, I started talking to her to learn more about her life, which I had not fully extracted in a month.

Ashlee's parents were divorced, and her dad had moved two states away. She missed him terribly. Her mother was now engaged to a man she didn't like. Ashlee had even thought of running away or somehow trying to get to her father.

I arranged to talk with Ashlee's mother to inform her of all this. She was appreciative, as she was unaware of her daughter's feelings. I'm not sure what happened, but a short time later, Ashlee stopped attending youth group. The rumor was that the family had moved out of town—perhaps to the father's state? I don't know.

Consider Ashlee's case compared to that of "Deena." When she was sixteen, Deena's parents had separated and reunited, but theirs was still a troubled marriage. Deena's father was not fully allowed to be her dad; the mother made sure of that.

Without that strong adult male role model, Deena found her own in her middle-aged band director. They began having an affair that lasted into her twenties. They nearly got married at one point before Deena had matured enough to move on.

When I was teaching a young adult class in my church, we got into a deep discussion of family life and the tangled relationships the young adults had, especially the women. Warring parents, abuse, absence, divorced situations— all of these had deeply affected these young women as they grew up and had continued to affect their adulthood.

At one point, I stopped the exchange to ask a question of each woman: "How close was your relationship to your dad at age thirteen to fifteen?" None of them who were speaking of their issues had a close relationship at that age. That deficiency had impacted all of them.

I then turned to the young men in the group. "I want you to hear what these young ladies are saying, and I want you to promise me something. If and when your daughter is thirteen to fifteen years old, you're going to be present for her. You are going to 'date' her so that you can affirm her. When she's sixteen, she's not going to need you so much anymore. But for those three years, you are the one to teach her what a woman is like and how a man should treat her. Promise me!"

The guys were confused but said yes. The women were both smiling and crying.

If you are a man reading this, please promise me, and yourself, that you will "date" your early teen daughter.

- You will assure her that she is worthy of the best attention by spending time with her (dates, meaning one-on-one activities), by listening to her, by being focused on her, and by building her up.
- You will assure her that she is beautiful, even when she points out her every flaw to you.
- You will show her how a man should treat her well, with respect, like a lady, and that she should expect this treatment from a man and settle for nothing less.
- You will show her how well a Christian man in particular can honor a woman.

If you are a woman reading this, you must promise me and yourself:

- You will encourage the father to do all these things above, with your full support.
- You will not undermine him in his attempts to execute this plan.
- Even if you are estranged, you will not bar a father from taking care of his daughter in this way, unless there is suspicion of or a history of abuse. *You not getting along with her father is not a sufficient reason.*
- If her father is not available, you will find a trusted male relative or friend who will fulfill this role in an honorable way.

My phrase that I have used so much in this book applies once more: you're doing all this "for the sake of the child."

Now that we've discussed preventative actions, let's identify follow-up, attentive actions in the next chapter.

Summary of Preventative Parenting

Key Points

- Be clear on your expectations regarding alcohol, cigarette, and drug use.
- Emphasize the "No blank check" policy: the teen cannot fill in their own decisions on outings without parental questioning and approval.
- Talk to teens after 11 p.m. in their bedroom to get maximum conversation. Trade off between parents as needed and if possible!
- A midpoint discussion during an evening outing is a way to offer flexibility while retaining oversight over teen outings.
- Be a host for your teen's circle of friends as often as possible, to provide a secure environment and to get to know them better.

Unison Parenting Foundation

- Form and enforce guardrails to prevent your child from becoming overscheduled.
- Become educated on drugs, alcohol, depression, teen sex, pornography, and other teen issues, and share findings with each other.
- Develop a family mission statement, core values, or other indicator expressing the family's values and how it functions.
- Arrange time for family togetherness, including one-on-one pairings of each parent with each child.
- Thirteen- to fifteen-year-old girls need a positive male role model, ideally the father. Remove any personal barriers that may block the father from accessing his daughter (excepting cases or suspicion of abuse).

Attentive Parenting

Meditation: Psalm 119:9

"How can a young person stay on the path of purity?
By living according to your word."

In our society, the word *purity* has come to be associated with sexual abstention. But that is not the biblical understanding of purity.

Biblical purity is holiness, not abstention. It is not the absence of something but the presence of something. Holiness means a setting apart, a commitment to act according to God's ways.

As you read these teen chapters, your inclination might be to get caught up in what you are trying to prevent. Instead, I want to emphasize again that we parents should be most interested in instilling the presence of something good, not solely enforcing the absence of something bad.

Even as I write about how to steer your kids clear of temptation, it's on my mind that we want to steer them toward God's ways, God's Christian community, positive goodness, and the light that can shine before others. Ultimately, instead of only instructing them to "Do not," we want to supplement this admonition with "Do" followed by a positive action.

Much of this book has been about *Do*, and now we're in a section of a lot of *Don't*s. Still, let's keep our eyes on the prize as parents. We want to raise good children into good adults who follow Jesus's Golden Rule of "Do to others what you would have them do to you."

May we parents also demonstrate that same positive action in our own lives, counterbalancing the world by behaving in accordance with God's Word ourselves.

Attentive Does Not Mean Oppressive

It's one thing to have a preventative approach to parenting your teens. It's another to follow up with attentive parenting.

Let's be clear: This is not helicopter parenting. This is not oppressive parenting. This is not dominant parenting. This is not suffocating parenting.

This is being attentive to what is going on with your teen and adopting specific policies and procedures to follow up on the rules laid out in the prior chapter.

I've broken this section into three parts: paying attention to yourselves (as parents), paying attention to your teen, and paying attention to other parents.

Paying Attention to Yourself

Let's face it, by the teen years, you can become pretty beaten down by all this parenting stuff. You may be subconsciously ready for the teen to fly away. You may even remember your own adolescence and wish you had had more freedom, so you might become lax in your parenting. Stamina, my friends!

> Refresh yourselves so that you can be attentive to your teen and what needs to be done to advance the concept of leading them to adulthood to become a functional, independent, well-prepared adult.

With your parenting partners, stay vigilant. Refresh yourselves so that you can be attentive to your teen and what needs to be done to advance the concept of leading them to adulthood to become a functional, independent, well-prepared adult.

Remember and reinforce the unison parenting pointers that have been presented in this book and hold each other accountable to your chosen parenting framework.

With that general statement said, let me highlight a few areas of specific attentiveness.

Don't Share Your War Stories

I recall an experienced drug counselor friend who hosted a parenting forum. She was asked what to do when children asked about your own use of alcohol or drugs, or your own experience with premarital sex, or other such questions. Her answer: "Lie!"

She explained that if you share any of your youthful indiscretions, you just gave permission to your child to do those things themselves. In her experience, the child thinks, "If Mom/Dad did this, and they survived, then it's OK to do."

If you're not comfortable with *Lie*, then I would say, *Deflect*. For example, say, "We're not discussing anything from my past. Good or bad, it's not useful to this discussion about you and what's going on today."

This may seem like a weak escape clause, but in my experience, if you stay on message, the questions will eventually go away.

218 | Unison Parenting

Do You Go or Stay Put?

There are a couple of situations that can happen when your child is at a party or social setting, and you get that parenting spider sense that something isn't right. Two situations require two solutions.

First is the sleepover request. From experience, I can tell you that you need to vigilantly respond to this situation: "Gee, Dad, I'm pretty tired. I don't feel like driving *(or walking)* home. Can I just stay over here for a sleepover? The other guys/girls are doing it, and it's OK with the parents."

I would say that, unless you have high trust in your teen, their friends, and the hosting parents, the answer should be, "No. You do not have permission. I'll come get you, and we'll pick up your car tomorrow." The reason is that the request may be an indicator that your child is drunk or will soon be.

Be strong. You're tired. I know you're tired or occupied or watching a movie in which you're really engaged. But this is an important moment. It's better if you have proactively decided with your parenting partner who will handle such a situation.

At minimum, I would ask for a parent at the party to be put on the phone or to call you so you can discuss the situation. But as we'll discuss later, you may not be able to trust them. So it's best to pull on your clothes and your shoes and pick up your teen, perhaps to their chagrin and perhaps to their future grounding, depending on the condition in which you find them.

An important point is that in this situation, the teen has asked for your permission, which is good, but has also invited your involvement by extension. They have inadvertently given you the right to get involved.

Here's a subtly different situation. Let's say you get the sense that something untoward is happening at the party. Or perhaps the hosting parent has had a history of questionable decision-making. Or maybe something in your child's texts during the evening gives you pause.

When you feel like something is wrong, you may have the inclination to visit to check out the scene. Don't.

I brought up this scenario at one of the teen panels in my parenting classes. I never did this myself but thought perhaps I should have on occasions when I didn't feel right about what might be going on at the party.

The teen panel was unanimous in saying that it was a huge breach of trust to show up at the party to check them out. You could potentially embarrass your child, which could lead to more rebellion and a compromised relationship. The panel recommended digging into the situation later with the teen and/or with the hosting family, being as private as possible in order to avoid embarrassing your teen in front of their friends.

Don't Try to Be the Cool Parent

Oh, this is a tempting one. I've said before that you want to host events when possible, but that doesn't mean you host in order to facilitate bad behavior.

I'll state clearly that you must not serve or allow alcohol to teens. First, it is illegal. Doug Rohan of Rohan Law points out:

> *If you host a party and alcohol is provided, you may be responsible for anything the teens do for the remainder of the night...Now your partygoers are leaving your house and possibly driving after using drugs or alcohol, or riding with a friend who has consumed drugs or alcohol. If someone is drunk or under the influence of drugs, you could be held liable for their actions even if you did not supply the substances.*[70]

Having alcohol available and absenting yourself might technically be a way out, but it's highly irresponsible. The logic you might be tempted to use is "They're going to experiment anyway, so they might as well do it in a safe place."

From my own parenting experience and from hearing other parental experiences, such parents do not provide a safe place! A horror story in our own community was when such a pair of parents looked the other way, thinking their house was a safe place, but they did nothing to create safety—in fact, they were drinking themselves and not paying attention to young people coming or going. They did not stop a pair of drunk teens from leaving in a car. One died; the other was paralyzed in the ensuing accident.

Don't look for wiggle room or how to create a "safe" atmosphere. You create a safe atmosphere by not permitting teen alcohol use in your home. Period.

Paying Attention to Your Teen

Let's pivot to talking about how to be attentive to your teen and what you're looking for. I'll say a few things that may run counter to what you're hearing from other parents

Actively Enforce Curfew

This topic is about being attentive to your child. But let's be clear: it also has to do with your own behavior, inclinations, lack of stamina, and prioritization.

I get it. You're tired. You want to go to bed. So does your parenting partner. But don't. At least one of you must be "on duty," staying up until the teen comes home, to ensure curfew was followed and to check on a few other things. Decide at the start of the evening which parenting partner has the night shift.

I can assure you that it was a deterrent to any misaligned behavior by the teenage me that I knew my father would be awake and waiting for me when I got home. The same went for my kids; either Mom or Dad was going to be greeting you when you got home, no matter the hour.

That helps with the time enforcement, but what else are you checking for?

- **You're checking their breath for alcohol.** And when I say checking their breath, I literally would get close to their face for a conversation. If everyone else was in bed, the better, as I could get closer to speak softly with the perceived intent of not waking up anyone else.
- **You're checking their eyes for signs of alcohol or drug use.** You'll just have to learn how their eyes look when they've had a night's worth of Red Bull while playing video games and how that is different from the look of illicit drug use. Whatever you have learned about substances of various kinds from prior chapter references, check for those things as well.
- **You're checking for general state of mind**, well-being, emotional distress, weariness, communicative ability, and so forth. Get their story on what happened during the evening and ask questions. Hopefully you have learned how your child generally behaves and communicates, so any warning signs will pop out.

The Pros and Cons of Tracking Devices

Technology has opened up more options for parental control. Family apps allow everyone to know the location of family members through their phones. There are tracking devices that can be affixed to cars. And probably a lot more that I haven't explored.

I will go on record that these are actually bad ideas for parental control, with exceptions I'll list later. There are two main reasons.

First, your teen can figure out how to game anything you come up with. If you put a tracking device on their car, and they figure it out, do you know what happens? They park the car where they're supposed to be, and they take someone else's car to where they want to be.

If their phone app indicates their location, then they will simply place the phone where they're supposed to be and go elsewhere. If you ask why they didn't answer your call or text, they have plausible deniability because of inconsistencies in our cellular networks. "Oh, the phone never rang," or "Oh, the text didn't come through until later."

I knew a couple that, for the reason of being fearful about their child driving on their own for the first time, tailed the teen's car to see how they were driving. Maybe the first time out, but still. Do you want to be that parent?

More control can definitely lead to more rebellion.

The second reason is that what you really want is a teen you can trust. In order to fully trust them, you should give them the chance to become trustworthy. Andrea Karin Nelson writes this in regard to tracking devices:

> *Ultimately, the goal as a parent is to raise our children to be self-sufficient adults. As hard as it is, giving them increasing freedom as they get older is vital to teaching them the skills they need to be on their own someday.*[71]

My recommended approach is to level with them from the beginning, making the following points:

- "I could use an app or a tracking device to know your whereabouts at all times. I think that you'll feel oppressed, belittled, and rebellious if I do that. Our goal is to collaborate, so I won't do that without good reason."
- "I want you to become a trustworthy teen who is as good as their word. I want to give you a chance to prove that you are trustworthy."
- "We have policies in place for how you achieve permission to go out and how to communicate with us regarding where you go or if something changes. Those are enough as long as you are a trustworthy person, so I don't need to track you."
- "You're almost always going to have someone you're accountable to. Right now, it's a parent. Later, it's a boss or a spouse or a roommate or a child or someone. It's important to develop and maintain trust with people, and that's what you're practicing with us as a teen."
- Returning to the phrase *without good reason*: "If you start giving me reasons not to trust you, then I'll have to reevaluate this policy. I hope we don't have to go there."

If we parents propose a context of collaboration and cooperation, then turn around and implement a policy of complete overview, our intentions and actions conflict. It is much more within the unison parenting philosophy to allow the child to prove their incremental decision-making ability.

A good option is that when your child is younger, you do use the apps for tracking. It's certainly appropriate for a ten-year-old with a phone or even a middle schooler. Then a rite of passage is to allow them to turn off the tracker (or remove it) as they grow older to indicate your growing trust and their growing independence.

Another pro of having a family app is when the teen wants it. I'm thinking of emergency situations or times when the teen might be lost and desires help finding their way home. At that point, the teen could turn on the app as part of seeking help rather than for you to mandate its use.

Finally, you should reserve the right to revisit your tracking device policy. For example, after a trust violation, you could mandate use of the app during a trust-building probation period. Recall the story of Brie, who left the school campus to visit a nail salon with her friend. The ensuing probation could've included the use of the app temporarily.

Ask No Questions—For Now

This recommendation is fairly well-known, but I'm not convinced that many parents actually practice it. You want the teen to be able to reach out to you when they've made a mistake, in order to get them home safely. It means that you pause asking any questions about why they got into the situation.

For example, your son is throwing up because he drank too much and now can't drive. Or your daughter tricked you and went to a party she wasn't allowed to attend but now realizes she needs to escape the party.

A policy that you should coordinate in advance of any incident is that you will pick them up (or otherwise help them escape to home) when they need it, no questions asked. At least not at the time. You'll wait twenty-four hours (or twelve hours, as an alternative).

This twenty-four-hour rule means that you focus on safety first and discipline later. You want to leave a safe path for your child to trust you to get them home without having to immediately face a tribunal.

Now, a teen still may not take you at your word. I would request in advance that they give you a chance to prove that you're trustworthy, just like you're giving them a chance through your parenting policies. But if they still don't want to trust you to get them home without a quarrel, then urge that they arrange a trustworthy friend or adult to assist them.

Get to Know Their Friends

You are giving your teen a lot more leash. It's only right to know who's at the end of that leash with your teen.

This doesn't have to be a friend interview, like a job interview. There are many ways to get to know their friends.

- **Ask questions about them**. These don't all have to come at once, either, but over time, you can ask things like:
  - What is Jeri like?

- What do you like about her?
- What is her family/home life like?
- What does she do outside of school?
- What are her future plans?
- These are all sincere, nonthreatening questions that can come up in the course of conversation.

- **Ask to be introduced**. Let's say that Tanner is coming over to pick up your child. Arrange for them to come in for a moment, or walk out to the car to meet them yourself. (I did a <u>lot</u> of the latter. By the way, they don't tend to peel out while you're standing there waving goodbye.)
- **Talk to them yourself**. Be willing to drive the group somewhere and strike up conversations (without trying to be the center of attention); even better, just listen while you're driving. Host events. Chat with them when you see them as you're picking up your child or attending a school event or performance. Invite them to dinner with your family.
- **Swap contact information**. There are very practical reasons to exchange contacts with your child's friends. What if your teen's phone dies? What if the group needs to reach you in an emergency?[72] Exchanging contacts doesn't mean you have to pepper them with texts. The way they react to your request can potentially indicate the kind of friend they are to your child.

At minimum, you're able to put a face with a name and know who your child is discussing as they relate stories of their day. (Remember, after 11 p.m.!)

At maximum, you'll be able to discern the influences these peers have on your teen and can more closely identify signs of either positive or negative influence.

Your teen may get frustrated with your desire to know their friends or their friends' parents. Psychotherapist blogger/podcaster Michael Ceely writes:

Remember, the idea is not to pry into all the details of your teen's social life. The idea is to assert your basic role as parent and know who your son or daughter is spending time with.... Your teenager may protest, and even accuse you of not trusting them. Stand firm. Your request is not unreasonable. Your kid may be mad at you, but deep down they'll respect you. A teenager needs certainty, and knowing that their parent has their back puts them at ease.[73]

Paying Attention to Other Parents

When a child is very young, their parents are tempted to run a background check on practically everyone who comes into contact with them. Yet when they become teenagers, parents find it hard to monitor all the interactions over a wider geographical area and basically give up.

However, the dangers that teens encounter are much greater than the dangers a preschooler may encounter, more life-changing, and more impactful on others around them too.

We parents can become lax about knowing the different parents our teens may encounter. We tend to assume that those parents have similar values, similar rules, and similar environments.

This is so far from the truth that it's frightening. In our case, the first ones to tell us this truth were actually our children. They indicated that other families functioned much differently than ours. Believe it or not, they began expressing an appreciation—even as teens—for the way we parented compared to peer parents.

You need to be attentive to how other parents behave. Here are a few things to consider.

Find Out about the Parents of Other Teens

Short of a background check, how do you do this?

- **Ask your teen**. Your teen is on the inside. What is the family structure? How does their household function, what rules do they have, and how does their family differ or match yours? Your teen can be a great source for this information, but you may have to coach their awareness.
- **Talk to the parents yourself**. This is harder than you might think. They may not be available when you are. They may not attend the

same school functions. If you are ever in the same room with them, such as at a school event, make it a point to meet and chat with them for a few minutes. If your parenting partner is with you, consider fanning out to meet as many parents as possible.

- **Find an excuse to interact with them**. Instead of your teen driving themselves, occasionally drive them yourself and meet the parents at their door. By phone or text or email, you can come up with a question about the event being held at their house and can arrange to contact them; anything to have a real conversation with them and see how they function. One mom wrote how her kids knew she would be asking for other parents' contact information and would provide it before being asked.[74]

- **Indicate that your house is a safe place for their child**. If their child will be visiting your house, you could check with a parent on anything you should know, including allergies. You could assure them that your house is going to be a safe place and share some of the rules you use to keep all the teens safe. Their reaction may tell you a lot about how they'll function as hosts. "Oh, you're not serving alcohol to the teens? Well, we would rather them learn about drinking in a safe place instead of out somewhere." Red flag!

- **Do things together as parents or as families**. Identify the high runners—the families your child is involved with the most—and work on those relationships. Invite the family to dinner or to meet a parent for coffee.[75]

If you wind up making new friends, great! But the first point is to understand the environment in which your kid will participate.

Beware of the Cool Parents

The same parent who gave me the 11 p.m. tip also expressed frustration with fellow church members who willingly gave teenagers alcohol at their house. He said, "I want to shake them by the shoulders and ask, 'What are you doing?'"

I've focused on alcohol so far, but that's not the only danger. Some parents do not insist on being present when teens are in the house. This was one of our rules, no matter the age of our children: a parent must be in the house when teens get together, whether at our house or another house. Admittedly, we had a couple of brief exceptions when Sara or I had to leave teens alone while picking up a younger child, but the time window was minimized, and the teens were reminded beforehand of our expectations for their behavior while we were gone.

A teen boy named "Patrick" learned the hard way how parents can even suggest or entice bad behavior. Patrick was dating "Lacey," whose parents had themselves had children at a young age and seemed eager for Lacey to do the same. The mother in particular would create situations where Patrick and Lacey could clearly be alone in the house and for Lacey to try to seduce Patrick. When Lacey's father caught them together in a compromising situation, a lot of things broke loose with both families. Patrick's parents had told him they didn't have a good feeling about Lacey's family, but love had blinded him. He found out on his own.

The main message is, once again, that you cannot assume other parents will abide by your rules or your points of view. Your teen may not have the experience or insight to understand other parents' motives, and besides, whatever they're suggesting may sound like a lot of fun. Dangerous fun, in reality.

What If You Don't Like What You Find?

I found this to be a tough question to answer myself as a parent. One of my children had a close friend that was a negative influence, in my mind. Protesting too much about the friend might drive my child away from me and toward the negative influence. Not speaking up would clearly lead my child down a bad path. In trying to tread the middle ground and let things play out but with governance, I still made a mistake that hurt my child's feelings and self-esteem—something I didn't discover until they became an adult.

This is such a delicate situation that you need to work together as parenting partners on how you will approach the situation.

The Parenting Teens & Tweens website lists several things to keep in mind when you don't like a child's friend, including:

- Realize that your child may be trying to help someone else, acting as a positive influence in their life. Don't rush your judgment; ask questions to understand the situation.

228 | Unison Parenting

- Be careful that you don't come across as not trusting your child's judgment. If you criticize their friend, the teen may take it that you are instead criticizing them.
- Try to understand what your teen gets out of the relationship. It may be possible to steer your teen to other activities or relationships—or even therapy—that will satisfy what they are trying to achieve.[76]

Probing, nonjudgmental questions are a parent's best friend.

Probing, nonjudgmental questions are a parent's best friend. I feel like if I had asked such questions more deftly, I could have handled my child's negative relationship differently. Even when your teen makes a statement that might startle you or with which you might disagree, it's usually best to start with questions to understand their thinking rather than simply knee-jerking a response to what they've said.

James Lehman shares another idea on EmpoweringParents.com of criticizing friend behavior rather than the friend themselves. He suggests clear, simple, recognizable comments such as:

- "I don't like that Jackie got arrested for shoplifting. I don't want you to get arrested for it, too."
- "Look, I'm sure your friends are great to you. But they all smoke pot, and they all get into trouble. If you hang out with them, you're going to get into the same trouble."
- "What are you trying to accomplish by letting people treat you this way? What are you getting out of that?"[77]

Hopefully you can tell from this chapter that proactivity is very important. Have a plan for attentive parenting, then execute it. When you encounter unusual situations, fall back on reactive parenting techniques of identifying, asking questions, and communicating with your parenting partner(s).

Summary of Attentive Parenting

Key Points

- Provide a safe, alcohol-free, drug-free space in your home. Don't be the cool parent, and beware of other cool parents.
- Don't use tracking devices or apps, as they undermine the trust you've built through collaborative parenting of your teen.
- Focus on safety in urgent situations, even if bad behavior was involved. Promise in advance to get them home safely and ask questions later. Request their trust in you, and stick to your promise.
- Get to know their friends and their friends' parents. Because of sheer volume at this age, you may have to select and meet high-runner friends and parents that seem to have the most interaction with and influence on your child.

Unison Parenting Foundation

- Develop an attentive parenting plan, as suggested by the points in this chapter, then consistently execute it.
- Figure out in advance who is handling the night shift, including going out to pick up the teen if necessary.
- Agree on your tracking device policy. My recommendation is not to use them on teens except in emergencies and during probation periods.
- When you don't like a friend in your teen's circle, discuss with parenting partners how to carefully approach the situation and coordinate actions, based on this book's recommendations.

A Final Thought

I didn't do it to be manipulative. I was absolutely sincere whenever I said it.

To a person, all my children told me, "It was devastating when you said that I disappointed you. I would rather you have yelled at me and gotten angry with me than to say that you were disappointed in me."

I told them, "But it was true. I was more disappointed than I was angry, and I just expressed that."

A manipulative parent would use that information to their advantage. I wasn't a manipulative parent.

In retrospect, I actually see my children's reactions as signs of love in our family.

I once heard the following statement about our relationship as God's children. I think it's true about that fatherly relationship, and it was true in my relationship with my children. The statement is:

> *People bound in religion repent for breaking rules.*
> *People walking in love repent for breaking their Father's heart.*

If we see God as the rule-maker and puppet master of our lives, we will be fearful of getting caught breaking rules. If we see God as the lover of our souls and the parent who perfectly blends discipline and grace, then we will be sorrowful for breaking God's heart with our behavior.

Similarly, if we see our parents as rule-makers and puppet masters, we'll walk on eggshells about breaking their rules. If we see our parents as loving and firm, then we will try not to grieve their hearts.

In retrospect, I can understand that my children saw me as their loving and firm parent. That's why disappointment was devastating. Not because of rules, but because of relationship.

I've given plenty of rules and advice in this book, but I hope that the rules have always come across as being wrapped in a loving relationship. I pray that you will wrap your rules in a loving relationship as well.

Please keep reading for three free offers designed to enhance your learning and your parenting.

Gratitude

I am grateful for the encouragers who helped me get to this point, either through their support of this book's development and/or through their support of Cecil Taylor Ministries. Specifically:

- My parenting partner, Sara Taylor. It wasn't always right or great or harmonious, but I'm incredibly proud of the adults that emerged from (and weathered) our parenting.
- Our children, Anthony, Austin, and Rebecca, for their love and their willingness to risk having a few of their stories told. Thank you for the "scroll" and all you have taught me as well. I'm so blessed to have you in my life!
- My own parents, Carl Taylor and Dorothy Taylor, who always seemed to treat me as a future adult rather than merely as a child.
- Official reviewers Kindra Silk Kreislers and Annette Marie Griffin for their time and their endorsement of this project. Kindra deserves special mention as she got involved in this project on the ground floor and was instrumental as a sounding board as I was writing the early chapters. She also created the free Choices Chart posters.
- Proofreader Megan Ryan for providing her expertise to create the best book possible.
- The team at Morgan James Publishing for how they loved this book from the beginning and for their patience in guiding me through their process.

- The parents who attended my parenting classes over a fifteen-year period and the parents I knew from my thirty-plus years of youth ministry. As I informed your parenting, your experiences have informed this book. Others will be blessed immensely as a result.
- The Cecil Taylor Ministries Prayer Team that walks with me each week through prayer, encouragement, and spiritual sustenance.

Finally, I am grateful to you for buying this book. I welcome your emailed feedback at **Cecil@CecilTaylorMinistries.com**, and I hope that you will accept one of the free offers so I can be in communication with you and help you further.

Please Review This Book!

Reviews are the lifeblood of an author. For the average author, like me, books simply can't be found and shared without people like you reviewing them.

Reviews, of course, help my book sales. But reviews also help fellow readers. They also help spread the message generally; if you find this to be a book others should read, you are spreading goodness by writing a review.

Please review this book! Regardless of where you purchased it, I would appreciate you visiting popular online book website(s) and leaving a review. You do not have to have purchased the book on that site, typically, to leave a review, although I understand that a famous one requires a small purchase amount over the past year if you didn't buy the book there. Even negative reviews are helpful, believe it or not, so say whatever you must.

People tell me they don't know how to leave a review. This process will vary slightly by book site, but generally speaking, here is the process:

1. Navigate to the book's page on the bookseller website.
2. Scroll down until you see the rating and reviews for the book. (Look for stars!)
3. Nearby, there will be a link to be able to leave a review yourself. Click on that link.
4. Typically you'll be asked to give a star rating, to create a review title, and to write a review. The review does not have to be long; only two

or three sentences are fine. But write all that you want beyond that, as longer reviews are helpful to create a picture for other readers.

5. Submit the review.

Thank you for your reviews. Thank you for sharing this book with others, either verbally or by handing them your copy. Thank you for posting about it on social media. Your effort will help someone else if you do.

About the Author

I was born into the family of a preacher and a teacher (eventually, after she raised four children). Those are the roots that have formed Cecil Taylor Ministries.

But those aren't the only roots. I feel like everything in my diverse life has led to this moment and to this ministry:

- My varied career in high-tech software development and product management, in sports broadcasting, and in running my own side businesses.
- Thirty-plus years in youth ministry, an adulthood of teaching adult Sunday school, and fifteen years of teaching parenting classes.
- Growing up in tiny rural towns, only venturing out of state once in my first twenty-three years, but eventually traveling to twenty-four countries on four continents.
- Being married for thirty-eight years and raising three children, one of whom was adopted.

- Working overtime many times but also experiencing unemployment or underemployment for nearly six years out of a ten-year stretch.

In other words, a little bit of almost everything. All those experiences inform my perspective in Cecil Taylor Ministries.

I'm going to tell you more about what I do in Cecil Taylor Ministries, but first let me tell you about who I am.

Someone once described me as a blend of serious and silly, which is an ideal mix for working with youth, by the way! I like to smile and laugh. Someone took a picture of me laughing in college, and my face was stretched out in a weird way. I commented on how strange I looked, but the person said, "But that's how you look!" I could live with that. I love to laugh.

I like to gently prank or fool people; I'm only searching for that singular moment of confusion that says, "Is this happening for real?" Then I let them in on what's happening.

I can be competitive, intense, driven, and fully Type A. I'm an extrovert who knows how to live with introverts. I don't know my scores for popular personality tests. I'm a natural leader and will fill a leadership void if one appears. I draw energy from people.

I've said (and have pretty much proven) that I can have a conversation with any stranger for five minutes. I genuinely like people, as frustrating as they can be. I will work the room at parties; actually, I've worked the room at funerals! I was recently at a wedding reception and told my wife Sara, "It drives me crazy to be in this room," and she knew why—I wanted to know everyone in the room, and it wasn't possible.

I am sure that I would love to talk to you someday.

As I pivot to Cecil Taylor Ministries, I must first point to God's call for me to be in this ministry. God is the CEO; I'm the COO. My external slogan is "Teaching Christians to live a seven-day practical faith," but my internal slogan is derived from 2 Chronicles 20:12: "I do not know what to do, but my eyes are on you."

The reason my ministry is focused on teaching Christians how to live a seven-day practical faith is that people would tell me after Sunday school classes, "I can do this Christian stuff on Sundays, but it's hard to do it the rest of the week." My goal is to help people live a daily faith, from Sunday to Sunday, not only because it honors God but because it helps fulfill Jesus's goal: that we may have life and have it abundantly.

I could spend much more ink on my ministry's books, video series, blogs, podcasts, video devotionals, speaking engagements, and so on. But instead, for current information on the Instant Content products and services available through Cecil Taylor Ministries, please visit **CecilTaylorMinistries.com**. Also see the book and video list that follows.

I pray that this book blesses your life and draws you closer to God. And I hope that I'm blessed to someday learn that it made a difference.

Free Offers and Additional Resources

Please explore these free offers from Cecil Taylor Ministries so you can go deeper into unison parenting study and practice. All these offers are available at the following link or via the QR code below.

https://www.ceciltaylorministries.com/free-gifts-re-unison-parenting

Choices Chart

If you liked the idea of the Choices Chart in the **Parenting Fundamentals** chapter, you may also like a Choices Chart of your own! There are two options.

The first is a specially designed version containing the same information as the Taylor family's Choices Chart. It spells out the seven Cs and the fruits of the Spirit. It also leaves room for you to add some of your own family information.

The second is a template for you to complete for your family. It leaves room for family guidelines or limits, room for family positive goals, and room for rewards.

Both are printable and just the right size for a refrigerator or bulletin board.

You can choose either one by following the link or QR code above. Simply register, and we'll email a Choices Chart to you.

Unison Parenting Workbook E-book

Every book and video study from Cecil Taylor Ministries includes the opportunity to go deeper in your study with the purchase of an accompanying workbook of some kind.

You can receive a **free copy** of the e-book (PDF) version of the *Unison Parenting Workbook* simply by registering at the link or QR code above. Cecil Taylor Ministries will then email you the free copy of the e-book.

If you prefer a paper copy, the printed workbook is available for sale on the Cecil Taylor Ministries store at **https://Store.CecilTaylorMinistries.com.**

Mini-Book on Fundamentals of Discipleship

Unison Parenting urges you to disciple your child—in other words, bring them up as disciples of Christ.

The **Formative Parenting** chapter puts special emphasis on this topic. But what is discipleship?

In this mini-book (e-book), I describe what discipleship is all about. It's based on a lesson from my parenting classes that I gave for fifteen years.

Consider this a first step in understanding how to disciple your child. Please check out my further offerings on discipling your child when you visit the link above, where you can register for the mini-book to be emailed to you.

Unison Parenting Monthly Newsletter

Keep in touch with the latest unison parenting information. Each month, you can receive unison parenting tips, read answers to parenting questions, and more. Cecil Taylor Ministries will deliver it to your email inbox.

Please follow the link or QR code to register.

Cecil Taylor Ministries Monthly Newsletter

Becoming a free subscriber to Cecil Taylor Ministries includes the following benefits:

- A monthly newsletter containing:
  - Tips and advice to strengthen individuals, small groups, and churches.
  - Ways your daily faith can be enhanced through Cecil Taylor Ministries' free content, such as blogs, devotionals, podcasts, and more.
  - Insider info on Cecil Taylor Ministries' activities.
  - A devotional to enlighten your faith.
- Occasional discount offers on Cecil Taylor Ministries products and services.

Follow the link or QR code to register. Selecting any of the other free offers automatically enrolls you as a free subscriber.

Books and Videos by Cecil Taylor

Unison Parenting is my fourth book and video series. Please check out these works as well:

From Comfort Zone to Trust Zone: How Jesus Urges Us to Take Leaps of Faith for His Kingdom looks at twelve Bible stories in which Jesus challenged people to go deeper in their faith, then interprets what Jesus intends for us today. The purpose is for us to continually evolve, following the restless Holy Spirit into new levels of trust and service. *Book and video study.*

Live Like You're Loved underscores the four biblical truths that you are loved by God, forgiven by God, sent by God into the world, and an eternal creature invited to eternal relationship with God. Then I outline sixteen memorable steps, called SAIL steps, that help translate that knowledge into a new lifestyle in which you live like you're loved, forgiven, sent, and eternal. *Live Like You're Loved* won The Well Christian Writers' Conference Oasis Award top prize for nonfiction. *Book and video study.*

The Next Thing: A Christian Model for Dealing with Crisis in Personal Life explores a four-part model for addressing any crisis using the central idea of facing the next thing in front of you. The work is deeply personal. *The Next Thing* won the Blue Lake Christian Writers' Conference Living Water Award as nonfiction runner-up and was also a finalist in the 2024 Christian Indie Awards (winners were not announced until after *Unison Parenting* publication). *Book and video study.*

Video series *The Legacy Tree: A Christian Model for a Life of Significance* identifies how you can define yourself, give yourself, and replenish yourself to provide significance for God's kingdom. Cecil uses a memorable metaphor of trees and their qualities to map into our lives and illustrate how, like a tree, we can achieve lasting significance. The series consists of twelve videos, which are available in three four-video packages for small group study. *Video study only.*

Books and videos are available at **CecilTaylorMinistries.com**. Books are also available from fine online booksellers.

Useful Links and QR Codes

Cecil Taylor Ministries Home Page:
https://www.CecilTaylorMinistries.com

Cecil Taylor Ministries Facebook Page:
https:// www.facebook.com/ceciltaylorministries

Cecil Taylor Ministries YouTube Channel:
https://www.youtube.com/channel/UCHP_khu3r77ubl5jvHsf5-w

Cecil Taylor's LinkedIn Page:
https://www.linkedin.com/in/ceciltaylor/

I've provided a page on my website containing useful links mentioned throughout the book. Please refer to this page to find those current links: https://www.ceciltaylorministries.com/unison-parenting-useful-links.

Endnotes

1   https://www.merriam-webster.com/dictionary/proactive

2   Chapman, Gary, et al. *The 5 Love Languages of Children: The Secret to Loving Children Effectively.* Woodmere, NY: Northfield Publishing, 2016.

3   Cantell, Krista. *Free Yourself from Anxious Attachment: A 3-Step System to Eliminate Insecure Thoughts, Doubts, and Jealousy to Get the Love You Deserve.* Independently published, 2023.

4   Smalley, Gary. *The Key to Your Child's Heart.* Dallas: Word Publishing, 1984.

5   Gerstner, Louis. *Who Says Elephants Can't Dance.* New York: Harper Business, 2003 reprint.

6   Nelson, Jane. *Positive Discipline: The Classic Guide to Helping Children Develop Self-Discipline, Responsibility, Cooperation, and Problem-Solving Skills.* New York: Ballantine Books, 2006.

7   "Motivation: Top Twenty Principles for Early Childhood Education," American Psychological Association, October, 2019, https://www.apa.org/ed/schools/teaching-learning/top-twenty/early-childhood/motivation.

8   Nelson, *Positive Discipline.*

9   Craft, Laine Lawson. *The Parent's Battle Plan.* Ada, MI: Chosen Books, 2023.

10 "40 Crazy Things Parents Say," Birute Efe, Playtivities, modified August 5, 2022, https://playtivities.com/40-crazy-things-parents-say/

11 Carolyn Hax column, *The Washington Post*, February 14, 2023, https://www.washingtonpost.com/advice/2023/02/14/carolyn-hax-parent-outsmart-toddler-tantrums/

12 "Early childhood brain development has lifelong impact," Arizona PBS, Last Accessed November 30, 2023, https://azpbs.org/2017/11/early-childhood-brain-development-lifelong-impact/

13 "The Teen Brain: 7 Things to Know," National Institute of Mental Health, Last Accessed November 30, 2023, https://www.nimh.nih.gov/health/publications/the-teen-brain-7-things-to-know

14 Baumrind, Diana. 1967. "Child Care Practices. Anteceding Three Patterns of Preschool Behavior." Genetic Psychology Monographs, 75: 43–83.

15 Maccoby, E. E., & Martin, J. A. (1983). "Socialization in the context of the family: Parent-child interaction." In P. H. Mussen (Ed.) & E. M. Hetherington (Vol. Ed.), HANDBOOK OF CHILD PSYCHOLOGY: VOL. 4. SOCIALIZATION, PERSONALITY, AND SOCIAL DEVELOPMENT (4th ed., pp. 1–101). New York: Wiley

16 Smalley, *Key to Your Child's Heart*.

17 "What's Your Parenting Style? ," Lauren Pardee, Parents, updated August 17, 2023, https://www.parents.com/parenting/better-parenting/style/how-your-parenting-style-can-affect-your-health/

18 "Will you parent like your parents? ," Alison Bowen, *Chicago Tribune*, last updated May 19, 2016, https://www.chicagotribune.com/lifestyles/parenting/sc-parent-like-your-parent-family-0524-20160519-story.html

19 "Authoritarian parenting style," Tracy Trautner, Michigan State University Extension, January 19, 2017, updated March 14, 2023, https://www.canr.msu.edu/news/authoritarian_parenting_style

20 "Characteristics and Effects of an Uninvolved Parenting Style," Kendra Cherry, VeryWell Mind, updated March 14, 2023, https://www.verywellmind.com/what-is-uninvolved-parenting-2794958

21 "How it Feels to Have Emotionally Neglectful Parents," Jonice Webb, Psych Central, June 21, 2020, https://psychcentral.com/blog/childhood-neglect/2020/06/how-it-feels-to-have-emotionally-neglectful-parents#1

22 Cantell, *Free Yourself from Anxious Attachment.*

23 "Which Parenting Type Is Right for You?," Donna Christiano, Health-line, September 27, 2019, https://www.healthline.com/health/parenting/types-of-parenting#takeaway

24 "Parenting Styles: A Closer Look at a Well-Known Concept," Sofie Kuppens and Eva Ceulemans, *Springer Journal of Child and Family Studies,* National Library of Medicine, September 18, 2018, https://www.ncbi.nlm.nih.gov/pmc/articles/PMC6323136/

25 "Permissive Parenting: New Research Reveals Effects on Child Development," Pamela Li, Parenting for Brain, accessed October 2, 2023, https://www.parentingforbrain.com/permissive-parenting/

26 Ibid.

27 Nelson, *Positive Discipline.*

28 Fletcher A, Steinberg L, and Sellers E. 1999. Adolescents' well-being as a function of perceived inter-parent inconsistency. Journal of Marriage and the Family 61: 300-310.

29 Liu, Q., et al. 2021. Positive Youth Development: Parental Warmth, Values, and Prosocial Behavior in 11 Cultural Groups. J Youth Dev. 16(2-3):379-401.

30 https://parentingscience.com/authoritative-parenting-style/

31 Smalley, *Key to Your Child's Heart.*

32 Kennedy, Rebecca, "Connect, Don't Fix," Try This at Home (blog), June 4, 2020, https://goodinside.com/blog/connect-dont-fix/

33 Chapman, Gary. *The Five Love Languages: How to Express Heartfelt Commitment to Your Mate.* Woodmere, NY: Northfield Publishing, 1992.

34 Nelson, *Positive Discipline.*

35 "The American Family Today," Pew Research Center, December 17, 2015, https://www.pewresearch.org/social-trends/2015/12/17/1-the-american-family-today

36 "U.S. Census Bureau Releases CPS Estimates of Same-Sex Households ," United States Census Bureau, November 19, 2019, https://www.census.gov/newsroom/press-releases/2019/same-sex-households.html

37 "Percentage of same-sex couples in the United States in 2022, sorted by children in the household," Statista, Last Accessed October 16, 2023, https://www.statista.com/statistics/325083/same-sex-couples-in-the-us-by-children-in-the-household/

38 "LGBT Parenting in the United States ," Gary J. Gates, UCLA School of Law Williams Institute, February, 2013, https://williamsinstitute.law.ucla.edu/publications/lgbt-parenting-us

39 "Grandparents Caring for Grandchildren
What Do We Know? ," Anne R. Pebley and L. L. Rudkin, Rand Corporation, 2000, https://www.rand.org/pubs/research_briefs/RB5030.html

40 "Grandparents Raising Grandchildren," Megan L. Dolbin-MacNab and Bradford D. Stucki, American Association for Marriage and Family Therapy, Last Accessed October 15, 2023, https://www.aamft.org/Consumer_Updates/grandparents.aspx

41 All of the studies cited in the bullets and paragraph were summarized and referenced in "Growing up with gay parents: What is the big deal? ," Richard P. Fitzgibbons, *The Linacre Quarterly,* National Library of Medicine, November, 2015, https://www.ncbi.nlm.nih.gov/pmc/articles/PMC4771005/.

42 "Behavioral Outcomes of Children with Same-Sex Parents in The Netherlands," Deni Mazrekaj, Mirjam M. Fischer, Henny M. W. Bos, Internal Journal of Environmental Research and Public Health, National Library of Medicine, May 13, 2022, https://www.ncbi.nlm.nih.gov/pmc/articles/PMC9141065/

43 "Children raised by same-sex couples do better in school, new study finds," Heather Long, *The Washington Post*, February 6, 2019, https://www.washingtonpost.com/business/2019/02/06/children-raised-by-same-sex-couples-do-better-school-new-study-finds/

44 "Kids Raised By Same-Sex Parents Fare Same As—Or Better Than—Kids Of Straight Couples, Research Finds," Robert Hart, *Forbes*, March 6, 2023, https://www.forbes.com/sites/roberthart/2023/03/06/kids-raised-by-same-sex-parents-fare-same-as-or-better-than-kids-of-straight-couples-research-finds/

45 Mishna, F., Pepler, D., and Wiener, J. (2006). Factors associated with perceptions and responses to bullying situations by children, parents, teachers, and principals. Vict. Offend. 1, 255–288. doi: 10.1080/15564880600626163.

46 "3 Parenting Tips for Same-Sex Couples (from a Child Psychologist & Parent Who Also Happens to Be Gay) ," Emma Singer, PureWow, July 5, 2022, https://www.purewow.com/family/parenting-tips-for-same-sex-couples

47 "Same Sex Parents and Their Children," Deanna Linville and Maya O'Neil, American Association for Marriage and Family Therapy, Last Accessed October 4, 2023, https://www.aamft.org/consumer_updates/same-sex_parents_and_their_children.aspx

48 Bretherton I. (2010). Fathers in attachment theory and research: a review. Early Child Dev. Care 180, 9–23. 10.1080/03004430903414661

49 "Untangling Caregiving Role From Parent Gender in Coparenting Research: Insights From Gay Two-Father Families." Nicola Carrone and Vittorio Lingiardi, *Frontiers in Psychology*, The National Library of Medicine, March 16, 2022, https://www.ncbi.nlm.nih.gov/pmc/articles/PMC8966119/

50 "Child development (3) - six to nine months," Better Health Channel, Last Accessed October 8, 2023, https://www.betterhealth.vic.gov.au/health/healthyliving/child-development-3-six-to-nine-months

51 Carolyn Hax column, *Dallas Morning News*, August 20, 2023.

52 Lewis, C. S. *Mere Christianity*. San Francisco: Harper Collins, 2001.

53 "Collaborative Problem Solving: Parenting Challenging Teens," Jason Drake, Katy Teen and Family Counseling, December 27, 2020, https://www.katyteenandfamilycounseling.com/post/parenting-challenging-teens

54 Ibid.

55 Smalley, *Key to Your Child's Heart*.

56 "Collaborative Problem Solving® (CPS)," Think:Kids, Massachusetts General Hospital, Last Accessed September 15, 2023, https://thinkkids.org/cps-overview/

57 "Collaborative Problem Solving: Parenting Challenging Teens," Jason Drake, Katy Teen and Family Counseling, December 27, 2020, https://www.katyteenandfamilycounseling.com/post/parenting-challenging-teens

58 Ibid.

59 Patterson, Grenny, McMillan. and Switzler, *Crucial Conversations, Second Edition: Tools for Talking When Stakes Are High*. New York, NY: McGraw Hill, 2011.

60 Ibid.

61 Paul Hersey and Ken Blanchard, *Management of organizational behavior: Utilizing human resources* 4th Edition. Hoboken, NJ: Prentice Hall, 1982.

62 "How to raise a spiritual child," Nancy Montgomery, BabyCenter, Last Accessed September 15, 2023, https://www.babycenter.com/toddler/development/how-to-raise-a-spiritual-child_1506133

63 "How to spiritually equip your children," Kristy J. O'Hara, World Vision, July 12, 2016, https://www.franciscanmedia.org/franciscan-spirit-blog/raising-spiritually-healthy-children/

64 "Raising spiritually healthy children," Alicia von Stamitz, Franciscan Media, May 13, 2020, https://www.worldvision.org/christian-faith-news-stories/how-spiritually-equip-children

65 "How fentanyl crept into North Texas and who is at risk from the deadly drug," Claire Ballor, Sharon Grisby, and Maggie Prosser, *Dallas Morning News*, September 2, 2023, https://www.dallasnews.com/news/2023/09/02/how-fentanyl-crept-into-north-texas-and-who-is-at-risk-from-the-deadly-drug/

66 "Gen Z more likely to report mental health concern," Sophie Bethune, American Psychological Association, January, 2019, https://www.apa.org/monitor/2019/01/gen-z

67 "Report Details How Gen Z Sees Themselves and Their Future; Explores Four Main Categories: Politics, School and Work, Technology and Culture, Family and Community," Walton Family Foundation, June 27, 2022, https://www.waltonfamilyfoundation.org/about-us/newsroom/report-details-how-gen-z-sees-themselves-and-their-future-explores-four-

main-categories-politics-school-and-work-technology-and-culture-
family-and-community

68   "Generation Z and Mental Health," The Annie E. Casey Foundation,
     Updated February 14, 2023, https://www.aecf.org/blog/generation-
     z-and-mental-health

69   "Why Gen Z Is More Open to Talking About Their Mental Health," Arlin
     Cuncic, VeryWell Mind, March 25, 2021, https://www.verywell
     mind.com/why-gen-z-is-more-open-to-talking-about-their-mental-
     health-5104730

70   "Hosting an Underage Drinking Party Could Be Costly to Your Liabil-
     ity," Doug Rohan, Rohan Law, December 14, 2022, https://rohanlawpc.
     com/hosting-an-underage-drinking-party

71   "To Track or Not to Track? Weighing the Pros and Cons of Using Loca-
     tion Tracking on Your Child," Andrea Karin Nelson, Bright Canary, April
     17, 2023, https://www.brightcanary.io/to-track-or-not-to-track-weighing-
     the-pros-and-cons-of-using-location-tracking-on-your-child

72   "New Friends and Old Pals: How to Handle & Interact with Your Teen's
     Friends Pt. 1," Tyler Wroblewski, Omni Youth Programs, April 19 2017,
     https://www.omniyouth.net/post/new-friends-and-old-pals-how-to-
     handle-interact-with-your-teen-s-friends-pt-1

73   "Parents: Do You Know Your Teenager's Friends? ," Michael Ceely,
     Michael Ceely Counseling, March 7, 2017, https://www.ceelycounseling.
     com/do-you-know-your-teenagers-friends

74   "Why I Insist on Knowing the Parents of My Teen's Friends," Grown
     and Flown, July 23, 2019, https://grownandflown.com/know-parents-
     teens-friends/

75   "New Friends and Old Pals: How to Handle & Interact with Your Teen's
     Friends Pt. 1," Tyler Wroblewski, Omni Youth Programs, April 19 2017,
     https://www.omniyouth.net/post/new-friends-and-old-pals-how-to-
     handle-interact-with-your-teen-s-friends-pt-1

76   "It's Hard When You Don't Like Your Teen's Friends–Here's How to
     Handle It," Parenting Teens and Tweens, Last Accessed September 10,

2023, https://parentingteensandtweens.com/how-to-handle-when-i-dont-like-my-teens-friends/

77 "Does Your Child Have Toxic Friends? How to Deal with the Wrong Crowd," James Lehman, Empowering Parents, Last Accessed September 10, 2023, https://www.empoweringparents.com/article/does-your-child-have-toxic-friends-6-ways-to-deal-with-the-wrong-crowd/

A free ebook edition
is available with the
purchase of this book.

To claim your free ebook edition:

1. Visit MorganJamesBOGO.com
2. Sign your name CLEARLY in the space
3. Complete the form and submit a photo of the entire copyright page
4. You or your friend can download the ebook to your preferred device

Morgan James
BOGO™

A **FREE** ebook edition is available for you or a friend with the purchase of this print book.

CLEARLY SIGN YOUR NAME ABOVE

Instructions to claim your free ebook edition:
1. Visit MorganJamesBOGO.com
2. Sign your name CLEARLY in the space above
3. Complete the form and submit a photo of this entire page
4. You or your friend can download the ebook to your preferred device

Print & Digital Together Forever.

Snap a photo Free ebook Read anywhere

Printed in the USA
CPSIA information can be obtained
at www.ICGtesting.com
JSHW020742100824
67883JS00002B/14

9 781636 984025